PostgreSQL Server Programming

Extend PostgreSQL and integrate the database layer into your development framework

Hannu Krosing

Jim Mlodgenski

Kirk Roybal

[PACKT] open source
PUBLISHING   community experience distilled

BIRMINGHAM - MUMBAI

PostgreSQL Server Programming

First published: June 2013

Production Reference: 1180613

Published by Packt Publishing Ltd.
Livery Place
35 Livery Street
Birmingham B3 2PB, UK.

ISBN 978-1-84951-698-3

www.packtpub.com

Cover Image by Hannu Krosing (hannu@2ndQuadrant.com)

Credits

Authors

Hannu Krosing

Jim Mlodgenski

Kirk Roybal

Reviewer

Gabriele Bartolini

Acquisition Editor

Sarah Cullington

Lead Technical Editor

Susmita Panda

Technical Editors

Veronica Fernandes

Vaibhav Pawar

Kirti Pujari

Amit Ramadas

Project Coordinator

Shraddha Vora

Proofreader

Joel T. Johnson

Indexer

Priya Subramani

Graphics

Ronak Dhruv

Production Coordinator

Arvindkumar Gupta

Cover Work

Arvindkumar Gupta

About the Authors

Hannu Krosing was a PostgreSQL user before it was rewritten to use SQL as its main query language in 1995. So, he has both the historic perspective of its development and almost 20 years of experience using it for solving various real-life problems.

Hannu was the first Database Administrator and Database Architect at Skype, where he invented the sharding language PL/Proxy that allows scaling the user database to work with billions of users.

Since leaving Skype at the end of 2006—about a year after it was bought up by eBay—Hannu has been working as a PostgreSQL consultant with 2ndQuadrant, the premier PostgreSQL consultancy with global reach and local presence in most of the world.

Hannu has co-authored another Packt Publishing book, PostgreSQL 9 Administration Cookbook, together with one of the main PostgreSQL developers, Simon Riggs.

> I want to sincerely thank my wife Evelyn for her support while writing this book.

Jim Mlodgenski is the CTO of OpenSCG, a professional services company focused on leveraging open source technologies for strategic advantage. He was formerly the CEO of StormDB, a database cloud company focused on horizontal scalability. Prior to StormDB, Jim held deeply technical roles at Cirrus Technology, Inc., EnterpriseDB, and Fusion Technologies.

Jim is also a fervent advocate of PostgreSQL. He is a member of the board of the United States PostgreSQL Association, as well as being a part of the organizing teams of the New York PostgreSQL User Group and Philadelphia PostgreSQL User Groups.

Kirk Roybal has been active in the PostgreSQL community since 1998. He has helped to organize user groups in Houston, Dallas, and Bloomington, IL. He has mentored many junior database administrators and provided cross training for senior database engineers. He has provided solutions using PostgreSQL for reporting, business intelligence, data warehousing, applications, and development support.

Kirk saw the value of PostgreSQL when the first small business customer asked for a web application. At the time, competitive database products were either extremely immature, or cost prohibitive. Kirk has stood by the choice of PostgreSQL for many years now. His expertise is founded on keeping up with features and capabilities as they have become available.

Writing a book has been a unique experience for me. Many people fantasize about it, few start one, and even fewer get to publication. I am proud to be part of a team that actually made it to the book shelf (itself an diminishing breed). Thank you Sarah Cullington from Packt Publishing for giving me a chance to participate in the project. I imagine that the PostgreSQL community will be better served by this information, and I hope that they receive this as a reward for the time that they have invested in me over the years.

A book only has the value that the readers give it. Thank you to the PostgreSQL community for all of the technical, personal, and professional development help you have given me. The PostgreSQL community is a great bunch of people, and I have enjoyed the company of many of them. I hope to contribute more to this project in the future, and I hope you find my contributions as valuable as I find yours.

Thank you to my family. Firstly, for giving me a reason to succeed. Also, thank you for listening to the gobbledygook and nodding appreciatively. Have you ever had your family ask you what you were doing, and answered with a function? Try it. No, then again, don't try it. They may just have you involuntarily checked in somewhere.

About the Reviewer

Gabriele Bartolini has been a long time open-source programmer and has been writing Linux/Unix applications in C and C++ for over 10 years, specializing in search engines and web analytics with large databases.

Gabriele has a degree in Statistics from the University of Florence. His areas of expertise are data mining and data warehousing, having worked on web traffic analysis in Australia and Italy.

Gabriele is a consultant with 2ndQuadrant and an active member of the international PostgreSQL community.

Gabriele currently lives in Prato, a small but vibrant city located in the northern part of Tuscany, Italy. His second home is Melbourne, Australia, where he has studied at Monash University and worked in the ICT sector.

His hobbies include calcio (football or soccer, depending on which part of the world you come from) and playing his Fender Stratocaster electric guitar.

Thanks to my family, in particular Cathy who encourages always something new to learn.

www.PacktPub.com

Support files, eBooks, discount offers and more

You might want to visit www.PacktPub.com for support files and downloads related to your book.

Did you know that Packt offers eBook versions of every book published, with PDF and ePub files available? You can upgrade to the eBook version at www.PacktPub.com and as a print book customer, you are entitled to a discount on the eBook copy. Get in touch with us at service@packtpub.com for more details.

At www.PacktPub.com, you can also read a collection of free technical articles, sign up for a range of free newsletters and receive exclusive discounts and offers on Packt books and eBooks.

http://PacktLib.PacktPub.com

Do you need instant solutions to your IT questions? PacktLib is Packt's online digital book library. Here, you can access, read and search across Packt's entire library of books.

Why Subscribe?

- Fully searchable across every book published by Packt
- Copy and paste, print and bookmark content
- On demand and accessible via web browser

Free Access for Packt account holders

If you have an account with Packt at www.PacktPub.com, you can use this to access PacktLib today and view nine entirely free books. Simply use your login credentials for immediate access.

Table of Contents

Preface

PostgreSQL is so much more than a database server. In fact, it could even be seen as an application development framework, with the added bonuses of transaction support, massive data storage, journaling, recovery, and a host of other features that the PostgreSQL engine provides. With proper knowledge in hand, you will be able to respond to the current demand for advanced PostgreSQL skills in a lucrative and booming market.

This book will take you from learning the basic parts of a PostgreSQL function through writing them in languages other than the built-in PL/pgSQL. You will see how to create libraries of useful code, group them into even more useful components, and distribute them to the community. You will see how to extract data from a multitude of foreign data sources, extend PostgreSQL to do it natively, and you can do all of this in a nifty debugging interface that will allow you to do it efficiently and with reliability.

What this book covers

Chapter 1, What Is a PostgreSQL Server?, introduces PostgreSQL's programming capabilities. It describes server programming and some of the real-world use cases that can leverage this technique.

Chapter 2, Server Programming Environment, discusses the PostgreSQL environment. It makes a case for why someone would choose to program in PostgreSQL covering some of PostgreSQL's business and technical advantages.

Chapter 3, Your First PL/pgSQL Function, introduces the PL/pgSQL stored procedure language. The basic structure of a function and some of the key building blocks are covered.

Chapter 4, Returning Structured Data, builds on the introduction to PL/pgSQL and shows how to return complex data back to an application. Several different methods are used and the pros and cons of each method is discussed.

Chapter 5, PL/pgSQL Trigger Functions, explores executing some server-side logic based on events occurring in the database. The concept of triggers is introduced and some use cases are discussed.

Chapter 6, Debugging PL/pgSQL, explores how server-side logic can be debugged. It starts with simple log-based notifications and builds to using an interactive graphical debugger.

Chapter 7, Using Unrestricted Languages, looks at writing server-side code in languages other than PL/pgSQL. It uses Python as the language of choice and covers reaching outside the database from a function.

Chapter 8, Writing Advanced Functions in C, provides an in-depth look at extending PostgreSQL with native C code. Several detailed examples are used to show the fundamental concepts of adding native PostgreSQL capabilities.

Chapter 9, Scaling your Database with PL/Proxy, covers another stored procedure language that allows PostgreSQL to expand beyond a single physical server. It discusses some techniques on how to split data to scale effectively.

Chapter 10, Publishing Your Code as PostgreSQL Extensions, discusses the PostgreSQL Extension Network and covers publishing a module out to the open source community.

What you need for this book

To follow along with the samples in this book, you will need the following software:

- Ubuntu 12.04 LTS
- PostgreSQL 9.2 Server or a newer version

Who this book is for

PostgreSQL Server Programming is for moderate to advanced PostgreSQL database professionals. To get the best understanding of this book, you should have a general experience in writing SQL, a basic idea of query tuning, and some coding experience in a language of your choice.

Conventions

In this book, you will find a number of styles of text that distinguish between different kinds of information. Here are some examples of these styles, and an explanation of their meaning.

Code words in text are shown as follows: "You can normally tell which type you're seeing by differences like this, whether you're seeing rows or RECORD."

A block of code is set as follows:

```
CREATE FUNCTION mid(varchar, integer, integer) RETURNS varchar
AS $$
BEGIN
  RETURN substring($1,$2,$3);
END;
$$LANGUAGE plpgsql;
```

When we wish to draw your attention to a particular part of a code block, the relevant lines or items are set in bold:

```
CREATE TRIGGER disallow_pk_change
AFTER UPDATE OF id ON table_with_pk_id
FOR EACH ROWEXECUTE PROCEDURE cancel_op();
```

Any command-line input or output is written as follows:

```
hannu=# select get_new_messages('50000');
```

New terms and **important words** are shown in bold. Words that you see on the screen, in menus or dialog boxes for example, appear in the text like this: "Click on the link **Upload a Distribution**."

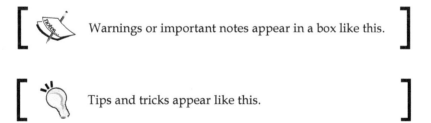

Warnings or important notes appear in a box like this.

Tips and tricks appear like this.

Reader feedback

Feedback from our readers is always welcome. Let us know what you think about this book—what you liked or may have disliked. Reader feedback is important for us to develop titles that you really get the most out of.

To send us general feedback, simply send an e-mail to feedback@packtpub.com, and mention the book title via the subject of your message.

If there is a topic that you have expertise in and you are interested in either writing or contributing to a book, see our author guide on www.packtpub.com/authors.

Customer support

Now that you are the proud owner of a Packt book, we have a number of things to help you to get the most from your purchase.

Downloading the example code

You can download the example code files for all Packt books you have purchased from your account at http://www.packtpub.com. If you purchased this book elsewhere, you can visit http://www.packtpub.com/support and register to have the files e-mailed directly to you.

Errata

Although we have taken every care to ensure the accuracy of our content, mistakes do happen. If you find a mistake in one of our books—maybe a mistake in the text or the code—we would be grateful if you would report this to us. By doing so, you can save other readers from frustration and help us improve subsequent versions of this book. If you find any errata, please report them by visiting http://www.packtpub.com/submit-errata, selecting your book, clicking on the **errata submission form** link, and entering the details of your errata. Once your errata are verified, your submission will be accepted and the errata will be uploaded on our website, or added to any list of existing errata, under the Errata section of that title. Any existing errata can be viewed by selecting your title from http://www.packtpub.com/support.

Piracy

Piracy of copyright material on the Internet is an ongoing problem across all media. At Packt, we take the protection of our copyright and licenses very seriously. If you come across any illegal copies of our works, in any form, on the Internet, please provide us with the location address or website name immediately so that we can pursue a remedy.

Please contact us at `copyright@packtpub.com` with a link to the suspected pirated material.

We appreciate your help in protecting our authors, and our ability to bring you valuable content.

Questions

You can contact us at `questions@packtpub.com` if you are having a problem with any aspect of the book, and we will do our best to address it.

1
What Is a PostgreSQL Server?

If you think that a PostgreSQL server is just a storage system, and the only way to communicate with it is by executing SQL statements, you are limiting yourself tremendously. That is using just a tiny part of the database's features.

A PostgreSQL server is a powerful framework that can be used for all kinds of data processing, and even some non-data server tasks. It is a server platform that allows you to easily mix and match functions and libraries from several popular languages. Consider this complicated, multi-language sequence of work:

1. Call a string parsing function in Perl.
2. Convert the string to XSLT and process the result using JavaScript.
3. Ask for a secure stamp from an external time-stamping service such as www.guardtime.com, using their SDK for C.
4. Write a Python function to digitally sign the result.

This can be implemented as a series of simple function calls using several of the available server programming languages. The developer needing to accomplish all this work can just call a single PostgreSQL function without having to be aware of how the data is being passed between languages and libraries:

```
SELECT convert_to_xslt_and_sign(raw_data_string);
```

In this book, we will discuss several facets of PostgreSQL server programming. PostgreSQL has all of the native server-side programming features available in most larger database systems such as triggers, automated actions invoked automatically each time data is changed. But it has uniquely deep abilities to override the built-in behavior down to very basic operators. Examples of this customization include the following.

Writing **User-defined functions** (**UDF**) in C for carrying out complex computations:

- Add complicated constraints to make sure that data in the server meets guidelines.
- Create triggers in many languages to make related changes to other tables, log the actions, or forbid the action to happen if it does not meet certain criteria.
- Define new data types and operators in the database.
- Use the geography types defined in the PostGIS package.
- Add your own index access methods for either existing or new data types, making some queries much more efficient.

What sort of things can you do with these features? There are limitless possibilities, such as the ones listed as follows:

- Write data extractor functions to get just the interesting parts from structured data, such as XML or JSON, without needing to ship the whole, possibly huge, document to the client application.
- Process events asynchronously, like sending mail without slowing down the main application. You could create a mail queue for changes to user info, populated by a trigger. A separate mail-sending process can consume this data whenever it's notified by an application process.

The rest of this chapter is presented as a series of descriptions of common data management tasks showing how they can be solved in a robust and elegant way via server programming.

The samples in this chapter are all tested to work, but they come with minimal commentary. They are here just to show you various things server programming can accomplish. The techniques described will be explained thoroughly in later chapters.

Why program in the server?

Developers program their code in a number of different languages and it could be designed to run just about anywhere. When writing an application, some people follow the philosophy that as much of the logic as possible for the application, should be pushed to the client. We see this in the explosion of applications leveraging JavaScript inside browsers. Others like to push the logic into the middle tier with an application server handling the business rules. These are all valid ways to design an application, so why would you want to program in the database server?

Let's start with a simple example. Many applications include a list of customers who have a balance in their account. We'll use this sample schema and data:

```
CREATE TABLE accounts(owner text, balance numeric);
INSERT INTO accounts VALUES ('Bob',100);
INSERT INTO accounts VALUES ('Mary',200);
```

When using a database, the most common way to interact with it is to use SQL queries. If you want to move 14 dollars from Bob's account to Mary's account, with simple SQL it would look like this:

```
UPDATE accounts SET balance = balance - 14.00 WHERE owner = 'Bob';
UPDATE accounts SET balance = balance + 14.00 WHERE owner = 'Mary';
```

But you have to also make sure that Bob actually has enough money (or credit) on his account. It's also important that if anything fails then none of the transactions happen. In an application program, the preceding code snippet becomes:

```
BEGIN;
SELECT amount FROM accounts WHERE owner = 'Bob' FOR UPDATE;
-- now in the application check that the amount is actually bigger
than 14
UPDATE accounts SET amount = amount - 14.00 WHERE owner = 'Bob';
UPDATE accounts SET amount = amount + 14.00 WHERE owner = 'Mary';
COMMIT;
```

But did Mary actually have an account? If she did not, the last UPDATE will succeed by updating zero rows. If any of the checks fail, you should do a ROLLBACK instead of COMMIT. Once you have done all this for all the clients that transfer money, a new requirement will invariably arrive. Perhaps, the minimum amount that can be transferred is now 5.00. You will need to revisit all your code in all your clients again.

So what can you do to make all of this more manageable, more secure, and more robust? This is where server programming, executing code on the database server itself, can help. You can move the computations, checks, and data manipulations entirely into a User-defined function (UDF) on the server. This does not just ensure that you have only one copy of operation logic to manage, but also makes things faster by not needing several round-trips between client and server. If required, you can also make sure that only as much information as needed is given out of the database. For example, there is no business for most client applications to know how much money Bob has on his account. Mostly, they only need to know if there is enough money to make the transfer, or more to the point, if the transaction succeeded.

Using PL/pgSQL for integrity checks

PostgreSQL includes its own programming language named PL/pgSQL that is aimed to integrate easily with SQL commands. PL stands for programming language, and this is just one of the many languages available for writing server code. pgSQL is shorthand for PostgreSQL.

Unlike basic SQL, PL/pgSQL includes procedural elements, like the ability to use if/then/else statements and loops. You can easily execute SQL statements, or even loop over the result of a SQL statement in the language.

The integrity checks needed for the application can be done in a PL/pgSQL function which takes three arguments: names of the payer and recipient, and the amount to pay. This sample also returns the status of the payment:

```
CREATE OR REPLACE FUNCTION transfer(
            i_payer text,
            i_recipient text,
            i_amount numeric(15,2))
RETURNS text
AS
$$
DECLARE
  payer_bal numeric;
BEGIN
  SELECT balance INTO payer_bal
    FROM accounts
```

```
        WHERE owner = i_payer FOR UPDATE;
      IF NOT FOUND THEN
        RETURN 'Payer account not found';
      END IF;
      IF payer_bal < i_amount THEN
        RETURN 'Not enough funds';
      END IF;

      UPDATE accounts
            SET balance = balance + i_amount
        WHERE owner = i_recipient;
      IF NOT FOUND THEN
        RETURN 'Recipient does not exist';
      END IF;

      UPDATE accounts
            SET balance = balance - i_amount
        WHERE owner = i_payer;
      RETURN 'OK';
    END;
    $$ LANGUAGE plpgsql;
```

Here are a few examples of using this function, assuming you haven't executed the previously proposed UPDATE statements yet:

```
postgres=# SELECT * FROM accounts;
 owner | balance
-------+---------
 Bob   |     100
 Mary  |     200
(2 rows)

postgres=# SELECT * FROM transfer('Bob','Mary',14.00);
 transfer
----------
 OK
(1 row)

postgres=# SELECT * FROM accounts;
 owner | balance
-------+---------
 Mary  |  214.00
 Bob   |   86.00
(2 rows)
```

Your application would need to check the return code and decide how to handle these errors. As long as it was written to reject any unexpected value, you could extend this function to do more checking, such as minimum transferrable amount, and be sure it would be prevented. There are three errors this can return:

```
postgres=# SELECT * FROM transfer('Fred','Mary',14.00);
        transfer
-------------------------
 Payer account not found
(1 row)

postgres=# SELECT * FROM transfer('Bob','Fred',14.00);
        transfer
-------------------------
 Recipient does not exist
(1 row)

postgres=# SELECT * FROM transfer('Bob','Mary',500.00);
      transfer
------------------
 Not enough funds
(1 row)
```

For these checks to always work, you would need to make all transfer operations go through the function, rather than manually changing the values with SQL statements.

About this book's code examples

The sample output shown here has been created with PostgreSQL's `psql` utility, usually running on a Linux system. Most of the code will work the same way if you are using a GUI utility like `pgAdmin3` to access the server instead. When you see lines like this:

```
postgres=# SELECT 1;
```

The `postgres=#` part is the prompt shown by the `psql` command.

Examples in this book have been tested using PostgreSQL 9.2. They will probably work on PostgreSQL version 8.3 and later. There have not been many major changes to how server programming happens in the last few versions of PostgreSQL. The syntax has become stricter over time to reduce the possibility of mistakes in server programming code. Due to the nature of those changes, most code from newer versions will still run on the older ones, unless it uses very new features. However, the older code can easily fail to run due to one of the newly-enforced restrictions.

Switching to the expanded display

When using the psql utility to execute a query, PostgreSQL normally outputs the result using vertically aligned columns:

```
$ psql -c "SELECT 1 AS test"
 test
------
    1
(1 row)

$ psql
psql (9.2.1)
Type "help" for help.

postgres=# SELECT 1 AS test;
 test
------
    1
(1 row)
```

You can tell when you're seeing a regular output because it will end up showing the number of rows.

This type of output is hard to fit into the text of a book like this. It's easier to print the output from what the program calls the expanded display, which breaks each column into a separate line. You can switch to expanded using either the -x command-line switch, or by sending \x to the psql program. Here is an example of using each:

```
$ psql -x -c "SELECT 1 AS test"
-[ RECORD 1 ]
test | 1

$ psql
psql (9.2.1)
Type "help" for help.

postgres=# \x
Expanded display is on
postgres=# SELECT 1 AS test;
-[ RECORD 1 ]
test | 1
```

Notice how the expanded output doesn't show the row count, and it numbers each output row. To save space, not all of the examples in the book will show the expanded output being turned on. You can normally tell which type you're seeing by differences like this, whether you're seeing rows or RECORD. The expanded mode will be normally preferred when the output of the query is too wide to fit into the available width of the book.

Moving beyond simple functions

Server programming can mean a few different things. Server programming is not just writing server functions. There are many other things you can do in the server which can be considered programming.

Data comparisons using operators

For more complex tasks you can define your own types, operators, and casts from one type to another, letting you actually compare apples and oranges.

As shown in the next example, you can define the type, fruit_qty, for fruit-with-quantity and then teach PostgreSQL to compare apples and oranges, say to make one orange to be worth 1.5 apples and convert apples to oranges:

```
postgres=# CREATE TYPE FRUIT_QTY as (name text, qty int);

postgres=# SELECT '("APPLE", 3)'::FRUIT_QTY;
 fruit_quantity
----------------
 (APPLE,3)
(1 row)

CREATE FUNCTION fruit_qty_larger_than(left_fruit FRUIT_QTY,
                                      right_fruit FRUIT_QTY)
RETURNS BOOL
AS $$
BEGIN
    IF (left_fruit.name = 'APPLE' AND right_fruit.name = 'ORANGE')
    THEN
        RETURN left_fruit.qty > (1.5 * right_fruit.qty);
    END IF;
    IF (left_fruit.name = 'ORANGE' AND right_fruit.name = 'APPLE' )
    THEN
```

```
            RETURN (1.5 * left_fruit.qty) > right_fruit.qty;
        END IF;
        RETURN  left_fruit.qty > right_fruit.qty;
END;
$$
LANGUAGE plpgsql;

postgres=# SELECT fruit_qty_larger_than('("APPLE", 3)'::FRUIT_
QTY,'("ORANGE", 2)'::FRUIT_QTY);
 fruit_qty_larger_than
-----------------------
 f
(1 row)

postgres=# SELECT fruit_qty_larger_than('("APPLE", 4)'::FRUIT_
QTY,'("ORANGE", 2)'::FRUIT_QTY);
 fruit_qty_larger_than
-----------------------
 t
(1 row)

CREATE OPERATOR > (
    leftarg = FRUIT_QTY,
    rightarg = FRUIT_QTY,
    procedure = fruit_qty_larger_than,
    commutator = >
);

 postgres=# SELECT '("ORANGE", 2)'::FRUIT_QTY > '("APPLE", 2)'::FRUIT_
QTY;
 ?column?
----------
 t
(1 row)

postgres=# SELECT '("ORANGE", 2)'::FRUIT_QTY > '("APPLE", 3)'::FRUIT_
QTY;
 ?column?
----------
 f
(1 row)
```

Managing related data with triggers

Server programming can also mean setting up automated actions (triggers), so that some operations in the database cause some other things to happen as well. For example, you can set up a process where making an offer on some items is automatically reserved to them in the stock table.

So let's create a fruit stock table:

```
CREATE TABLE fruits_in_stock (
    name text PRIMARY KEY,
    in_stock integer NOT NULL,
    reserved integer NOT NULL DEFAULT 0,
    CHECK (in_stock between 0 and 1000 ),
    CHECK (reserved <= in_stock)
);
```

The CHECK constraints make sure that some basic rules are followed: you can't have more than 1000 fruits in stock (they'll probably go bad), you can't have negative stock, and you can't reserve more than what you have.

```
CREATE TABLE fruit_offer (
    offer_id serial PRIMARY KEY,
    recipient_name text,
    offer_date timestamp default current_timestamp,
    fruit_name text REFERENCES fruits_in_stock,
    offered_amount integer
);
```

The offer table has an ID for the offer (so you can distinguish between offers later), recipient, date, offered fruit name, and offered amount.

For automating the reservation management, you first need a TRIGGER function, which implements the management logic:

```
CREATE OR REPLACE FUNCTION reserve_stock_on_offer () RETURNS trigger
AS $$
    BEGIN
        IF TG_OP = 'INSERT' THEN
            UPDATE fruits_in_stock
          SET reserved = reserved + NEW.offered_amount
        WHERE name = NEW.fruit_name;
    ELSIF TG_OP = 'UPDATE' THEN
        UPDATE fruits_in_stock
            SET reserved = reserved - OLD.offered_amount
                                    + NEW.offered_amount
```

```
        WHERE name = NEW.fruit_name;
    ELSIF TG_OP = 'DELETE' THEN
        UPDATE fruits_in_stock
            SET reserved = reserved - OLD.offered_amount
        WHERE name = OLD.fruit_name;
            END IF;
            RETURN NEW;
        END;
    $$ LANGUAGE plpgsql;
```

You have to tell PostgreSQL to call this function each and every time the offer row is changed:

```
CREATE TRIGGER manage_reserve_stock_on_offer_change
AFTER INSERT OR UPDATE OR DELETE ON fruit_offer
    FOR EACH ROW EXECUTE PROCEDURE reserve_stock_on_offer();
```

After this we are ready to test the functionality. First, we will add some fruit to our stock:

```
INSERT INTO fruits_in_stock(name,in_stock)
```

Then, we check that stock (this is using the expanded display):

```
postgres=# \x
Expanded display is on.
postgres=# SELECT * FROM fruits_in_stock;
-[ RECORD 1 ]----
name     | APPLE
in_stock | 500
reserved | 0
-[ RECORD 2 ]----
name     | ORANGE
in_stock | 500
reserved | 0
```

Next, let's make an offer of 100 apples to Bob:

```
postgres=# INSERT INTO fruit_offer(recipient_name,fruit_name,offered_
amount) VALUES('Bob','APPLE',100);
INSERT 0 1
postgres=# SELECT * FROM fruit_offer;
-[ RECORD 1 ]--+--------------------------
offer_id       | 1
recipient_name | Bob
offer_date     | 2013-01-25 15:21:15.281579
fruit_name     | APPLE
```

```
offered_amount | 100

postgres=# SELECT * FROM fruits_in_stock;
-[ RECORD 1 ]----
name     | ORANGE
in_stock | 500
reserved | 0
-[ RECORD 2 ]----
name     | APPLE
in_stock | 500
reserved | 100
```

On checking the stock we see that indeed 100 apples are reserved:

```
postgres=# SELECT * FROM fruits_in_stock;
-[ RECORD 1 ]----
name     | ORANGE
in_stock | 500
reserved | 0
-[ RECORD 2 ]----
name     | APPLE
in_stock | 500
reserved | 100
```

If we change the offered amount, the reservation follows:

```
postgres=# UPDATE fruit_offer SET offered_amount = 115 WHERE offer_id
= 1;
UPDATE 1
postgres=# SELECT * FROM fruits_in_stock;
-[ RECORD 1 ]----
name     | ORANGE
in_stock | 500
reserved | 0
-[ RECORD 2 ]----
name     | APPLE
in_stock | 500
reserved | 115
```

We also get some extra benefits. First, because of the constraint on the stock table, you can't sell the reserved apples:

```
postgres=# UPDATE fruits_in_stock SET in_stock = 100 WHERE name =
'APPLE';
ERROR:  new row for relation "fruits_in_stock" violates check
constraint "fruits_in_stock_check"
DETAIL:  Failing row contains (APPLE, 100, 115).
```

More interestingly, you also can't reserve more than you have, even though the constraints are on another table:

```
postgres=# UPDATE fruit_offer SET offered_amount = 1100 WHERE offer_id
= 1;
ERROR:  new row for relation "fruits_in_stock" violates check
constraint "fruits_in_stock_check"
DETAIL:  Failing row contains (APPLE, 500, 1100).
CONTEXT:  SQL statement "UPDATE fruits_in_stock
        SET reserved = reserved - OLD.offered_amount
                                     + NEW.offered_amount
      WHERE name = NEW.fruit_name"
PL/pgSQL function reserve_stock_on_offer() line 8 at SQL statement
```

When you finally delete the offer, the reservation is released:

```
postgres=# DELETE FROM fruit_offer WHERE offer_id = 1;
DELETE 1
postgres=# SELECT * FROM fruits_in_stock;
-[ RECORD 1 ]----
name     | ORANGE
in_stock | 500
reserved | 0
-[ RECORD 2 ]----
name     | APPLE
in_stock | 500
reserved | 0
```

In a real system, you probably would archive the old offer before deleting it.

Auditing changes

If you need to know who did what to the data and when it was done, one way to do that is to log every action that is performed on an important table.

There are at least two equally valid ways of doing the auditing:

- Use auditing triggers
- Allow tables to be accessed only through functions, and do the auditing inside these functions

Here, we will take a look at minimal examples of both the approaches.

First, let's create the tables:

```
CREATE TABLE salaries(
    emp_name text PRIMARY KEY,
    salary integer NOT NULL
);

CREATE TABLE salary_change_log(
    changed_by text DEFAULT CURRENT_USER,
    changed_at timestamp DEFAULT CURRENT_TIMESTAMP,
    salary_op text,
    emp_name text,
    old_salary integer,
    new_salary integer
);
REVOKE ALL ON salary_change_log FROM PUBLIC;
GRANT ALL ON salary_change_log TO managers;
```

You don't generally want your users to be able to change audit logs, so grant only the managers the right to access these. If you plan to let users access the salary table directly, you should put a trigger on it for auditing:

```
CREATE OR REPLACE FUNCTION log_salary_change () RETURNS trigger AS $$
    BEGIN
        IF TG_OP = 'INSERT' THEN
         INSERT INTO salary_change_log(salary_op,emp_name,new_salary)
         VALUES (TG_OP,NEW.emp_name,NEW.salary);
   ELSIF TG_OP = 'UPDATE' THEN         INSERT INTO salary_change_
log(salary_op,emp_name,old_salary,new_salary)
         VALUES (TG_OP,NEW.emp_name,OLD.salary,NEW.salary);
   ELSIF TG_OP = 'DELETE' THEN
        INSERT INTO salary_change_log(salary_op,emp_name,old_salary)
        VALUES (TG_OP,NEW.emp_name,OLD.salary);
        END IF;
        RETURN NEW;
    END;
$$ LANGUAGE plpgsql SECURITY DEFINER;

CREATE TRIGGER audit_salary_change
AFTER INSERT OR UPDATE OR DELETE ON salaries
    FOR EACH ROW EXECUTE PROCEDURE log_salary_change ();
```

Now, let's test out some salary management:

```
postgres=# INSERT INTO salaries values('Bob',1000);
INSERT 0 1
postgres=# UPDATE salaries set salary = 1100 where emp_name = 'Bob';
UPDATE 1
postgres=# INSERT INTO salaries values('Mary',1000);
INSERT 0 1
postgres=# UPDATE salaries set salary = salary + 200;
UPDATE 2
postgres=# SELECT * FROM salaries;
-[ RECORD 1 ]--
emp_name | Bob
salary   | 1300
-[ RECORD 2 ]--
emp_name | Mary
salary   | 1200
```

Each one of those changes is saved into the salary change log table for auditing purposes:

```
postgres=# SELECT * FROM salary_change_log;
-[ RECORD 1 ]-------------------------
changed_by | frank
changed_at | 2012-01-25 15:44:43.311299
salary_op  | INSERT
emp_name   | Bob
old_salary |
new_salary | 1000
-[ RECORD 2 ]-------------------------
changed_by | frank
changed_at | 2012-01-25 15:44:43.313405
salary_op  | UPDATE
emp_name   | Bob
old_salary | 1000
new_salary | 1100
-[ RECORD 3 ]-------------------------
changed_by | frank
changed_at | 2012-01-25 15:44:43.314208
salary_op  | INSERT
emp_name   | Mary
old_salary |
new_salary | 1000
-[ RECORD 4 ]-------------------------
changed_by | frank
```

```
changed_at  | 2012-01-25 15:44:43.314903
salary_op   | UPDATE
emp_name    | Bob
old_salary  | 1100
new_salary  | 1300
-[ RECORD 5 ]------------------------
changed_by  | frank
changed_at  | 2012-01-25 15:44:43.314903
salary_op   | UPDATE
emp_name    | Mary
old_salary  | 1000new_salary | 1200
```

On the other hand, you may not want anybody to have direct access to the salary table, in which case you can perform the following:

```
REVOKE ALL ON salaries FROM PUBLIC;
```

Also, give users access to only two functions: the first is for any user looking at salaries and the other is for changing salaries, which is available only to managers.

The functions themselves will have all the access to underlying tables because they are declared as SECURITY DEFINER, which means they run with the privileges of the user who created them.

The salary lookup function will look like the following:

```
CREATE OR REPLACE FUNCTION get_salary(text)
RETURNS integer
AS $$
    -- if you look at other people's salaries, it gets logged
    INSERT INTO salary_change_log(salary_op,emp_name,new_salary)
    SELECT 'SELECT',emp_name,salary
      FROM salaries
     WHERE upper(emp_name) = upper($1)
        AND upper(emp_name) != upper(CURRENT_USER); - don't log select
of own salary
    -- return the requested salary
    SELECT salary FROM salaries WHERE upper(emp_name) = upper($1);
$$ LANGUAGE SQL SECURITY DEFINER;
```

Notice that we implemented a "soft security" approach, where you can look up for other people's salaries, but you have to do it responsibly, that is, only when you need to as your manager will know that you have checked.

The `set_salary()` function abstracts away the need to check if the user exists; if the user does not, it is created. Setting someone's salary to `0` will remove him from the salary table. Thus, the interface is much simplified and the client application of these functions needs to know and do less:

```
CREATE OR REPLACE FUNCTION set_salary(i_emp_name text, i_salary int)
RETURNS TEXT AS $$
DECLARE
    old_salary integer;
BEGIN
    SELECT salary INTO old_salary
      FROM salaries
     WHERE upper(emp_name) = upper(i_emp_name);
    IF NOT FOUND THEN
        INSERT INTO salaries VALUES(i_emp_name, i_salary);
   INSERT INTO salary_change_log(salary_op,emp_name,new_salary)
      VALUES ('INSERT',i_emp_name,i_salary);
        RETURN 'INSERTED USER ' || i_emp_name;
    ELSIF i_salary > 0 THEN
        UPDATE salaries
     SET salary = i_salary
   WHERE upper(emp_name) = upper(i_emp_name);
   INSERT INTO salary_change_log
                (salary_op,emp_name,old_salary,new_salary)
      VALUES ('UPDATE',i_emp_name,old_salary,i_salary);
        RETURN 'UPDATED USER ' || i_emp_name;
    ELSE -- salary set to 0
        DELETE FROM salaries WHERE upper(emp_name) = upper(i_emp_
name);
   INSERT INTO salary_change_log(salary_op,emp_name,old_salary)
      VALUES ('DELETE',i_emp_name,old_salary);
        RETURN 'DELETED USER ' || i_emp_name;
    END IF;
END;
$$ LANGUAGE plpgsql SECURITY DEFINER;
```

Now, drop the `audit` trigger (or the changes will be logged twice) and test the new functionality:

```
postgres=# DROP TRIGGER audit_salary_change ON salaries;
DROP TRIGGER
postgres=#
postgres=# SELECT set_salary('Fred',750);
-[ RECORD 1 ]------------------
```

```
set_salary | INSERTED USER Fred

postgres=# SELECT set_salary('frank',100);
-[ RECORD 1 ]-------------------
set_salary | INSERTED USER frank

postgres=# SELECT * FROM salaries ;
-[ RECORD 1 ]---
emp_name | Bob
salary   | 1300
-[ RECORD 2 ]---
emp_name | Mary
salary   | 1200
-[ RECORD 3 ]---
emp_name | Fred
salary   | 750
-[ RECORD 4 ]---
emp_name | frank
salary   | 100

postgres=# SELECT set_salary('mary',0);
-[ RECORD 1 ]-----------------
set_salary | DELETED USER mary

postgres=# SELECT * FROM salaries ;
-[ RECORD 1 ]---
emp_name | Bob
salary   | 1300
-[ RECORD 2 ]---
emp_name | Fred
salary   | 750
-[ RECORD 3 ]---
emp_name | frank
salary   | 100

postgres=# SELECT * FROM salary_change_log ;
...
-[ RECORD 6 ]-------------------------
changed_by | gsmith
changed_at | 2013-01-25 15:57:49.057592
salary_op  | INSERT
emp_name   | Fred
old_salary |
new_salary | 750
```

```
-[ RECORD 7 ]-------------------------
changed_by | gsmith
changed_at | 2013-01-25 15:57:49.062456
salary_op  | INSERT
emp_name   | frank
old_salary |
new_salary | 100
-[ RECORD 8 ]-------------------------
changed_by | gsmith
changed_at | 2013-01-25 15:57:49.064337
salary_op  | DELETE
emp_name   | mary
old_salary | 1200
new_salary |
```

Data cleaning

We notice that employee names don't have consistent cases. It would be easy to enforce consistency by adding a constraint.

```
CHECK (emp_name = upper(emp_name))
```

However, it is even better to just make sure that it is stored as uppercase, and the simplest way to do it is by using trigger:

```
CREATE OR REPLACE FUNCTION uppercase_name ()
  RETURNS trigger AS $$
    BEGIN
        NEW.emp_name = upper(NEW.emp_name);
        RETURN NEW;
    END;
$$ LANGUAGE plpgsql;

CREATE TRIGGER uppercase_emp_name
BEFORE INSERT OR UPDATE OR DELETE ON salaries
    FOR EACH ROW EXECUTE PROCEDURE uppercase_name ();
```

The next set_salary() call for a new employee will now insert emp_name in uppercase:

```
postgres=# SELECT set_salary('arnold',80);
-[ RECORD 1 ]-------------------
set_salary | INSERTED USER arnold
```

As the uppercasing happened inside a trigger, the function response still shows a lowercase name, but in the database it is uppercase:

```
postgres=# SELECT * FROM salaries ;
-[ RECORD 1 ]---
emp_name | Bob
salary   | 1300
-[ RECORD 2 ]---
emp_name | Fred
salary   | 750
-[ RECORD 3 ]---
emp_name | frank
salary   | 100
-[ RECORD 4 ]---
emp_name |  ARNOLD
salary   | 80
```

After fixing the existing mixed-case emp_names, we can make sure that all emp_names will be in uppercase in the future by adding a constraint:

```
postgres=# update salaries set emp_name = upper(emp_name) where not
emp_name = upper(emp_name);
UPDATE 3
postgres=# alter table salaries add constraint emp_name_must_be_
uppercasepostgres-# CHECK (emp_name = upper(emp_name));
ALTER TABLE
```

If this behavior is needed in more places, it would make sense to define a new type – say u_text, which is always stored as uppercase. You will learn more about this approach in the chapter about defining user types.

Custom sort orders

The last example in this chapter is about using functions for different ways of sorting.

Say we are given a task of sorting words by their vowels only, and in addition to that, make the last vowel the most significant one when sorting. While this task may seem really complicated at first, it is easy to solve with functions:

```
CREATE OR REPLACE FUNCTION reversed_vowels(word text)
   RETURNS text AS $$
 vowels = [c for c in word.lower() if c in 'aeiou']
 vowels.reverse()
 return ''.join(vowels)
```

```
$$ LANGUAGE plpythonu IMMUTABLE;

postgres=# select word,reversed_vowels(word) from words order by
reversed_vowels(word);
    word     | reversed_vowels
-------------+-----------------
 Abracadabra | aaaaa
 Great       | ae
 Barter      | ea
 Revolver    | eoe
(4 rows)
```

The best part is that you can use your new function in an index definition:

```
postgres=# CREATE INDEX reversed_vowels_index ON words (reversed_
vowels(word));
CREATE INDEX
```

The system will automatically use this index whenever the function
reversed_vowels(word) is used in the WHERE clause or ORDER BY.

Programming best practices

Developing application software is complicated. Some of the approaches to help
manage that complexity are so popular that they've been given simple acronyms to
remember them. Next, we'll introduce some of these principles and show how server
programming helps make them easier to follow.

KISS – keep it simple stupid

One of the main techniques to successful programming is writing simple code.
That is, writing code that you can easily understand three years from now, and
that others can understand as well. It is not always achievable, but it almost always
makes sense to write your code in the simplest way possible. You may rewrite parts
of it later for various reasons such as speed, code compactness, to show off how
clever you are, and so on. But always write the code first in a simple way, so you can
absolutely be sure that it does what you want. Not only do you get working on code
fast, you also have something to compare to when you try more advanced ways to
do the same thing.

And remember, debugging is harder than writing code; so if you write the code in
the most complex way you can, you will have a really hard time debugging it.

It is often easier to write a set returning function instead of a complex query. Yes, it will probably run slower than the same thing implemented as a single complex query due to the fact that the optimizer can do very little to code written as functions, but the speed may be sufficient for your needs. If more speed is needed, it's very likely to refactor the code piece by piece, joining parts of the function into larger queries where the optimizer has a better chance of discovering better query plans until the performance is acceptable again.

Remember that for most of the times, you don't need the absolutely fastest code. For your clients or bosses, the best code is the one that does the job well and arrives on time.

DRY – don't repeat yourself

This one means to try to implement any piece of business logic just once, and put the code for doing it in the right place.

It may sometimes be hard, for example you do want to do some checking of your web forms in the browser, but still do the final check in the database. But as a general guideline it is very much valid.

Server programming helps a lot here. If your data manipulation code is in the database near the data, all the data users have easy access to it, and you will not need to manage a similar code in a C++ Windows program, two PHP websites, and a bunch of Python scripts doing nightly management tasks. If any of them needs to do this thing to a customer's table, they just call:

```
SELECT * FROM  do_this_thing_to_customers(arg1, arg2, arg3);
```

And that's it!

If the logic behind the function needs changing, you just change the function with no downtime and no complicated orchestration of pushing database query updates to several clients. Once the function is changed in the database, it is changed for all users.

YAGNI – you ain't gonna need it

In other words, don't do more than you absolutely need to.

If you have a creepy feeling that your client is not yet well aware of what the final database will look like or what it will do, it's helpful to resist the urge to design "everything" into the database. A much better way is to do the minimal implementation that satisfies the current spec, but do it with extensibility in mind. It is much easier to "paint yourself into a corner" when implementing a big spec with large imaginary parts.

If you organize your access to the database through functions, it is often possible to do even large rewrites of business logic without touching the frontend application code. Your application still does SELECT * FROM do_this_thing_to_ customers(arg1, arg2, arg3) even after you have rewritten the function five times and changed the whole table structure twice.

SOA – service-oriented architecture

Usually when you hear the acronym SOA, it comes from Enterprise Software people selling you a complex set of SOAP services. But the essence of the SOA is organizing your software platform as a set of services that clients and other services call for performing certain well-defined atomic tasks, such as:

- Checking a user's password and credentials
- Presenting him/her with a list of his/her favorite websites
- Selling him/her a new red dog collar with complementary membership in the red-collared dog club

These services can be implemented as SOAP calls with corresponding WSDL definitions and Java servers with servlet containers, and complex management infrastructure. They can also be a set of PostgreSQL functions, taking a set of arguments and returning a set of values. If arguments or return values are complex, they can be passed as XML or JSON, but often a simple set of standard PostgreSQL data types is enough. In *Chapter 9, Scaling Your Database with PL/Proxy*, we will learn how to make such PostgreSQL-based SOA service infinitely scalable.

Type extensibility

Some of the preceding techniques are available in other databases, but PostgreSQL's extensibility does not stop here. In PostgreSQL, you can just write User-defined functions (UDFs) in any of the most popular scripting languages. You can also define your own types, not just domains, which are standard types with some extra constraints attached, but new full-fledged types too.

For example, a Dutch company MGRID has developed **value with unit** set of data types, so that you can divide 10 km by 0.2 hour and get the result in 50 km/h. Of course, you can also cast the same result to meters per second or any other unit of speed. And yes, you can get this as a fraction of **c** — the speed of light.

This kind of functionality needs both the types themselves and overloaded operands, which know that if you divide distance by time then the result is speed. You will also need user-defined casts, which are automatically- or manually-invoked conversion functions between types.

MGRID developed this for use in medical applications where the cost of error can be high—the difference between 10 ml and 10 cc can be vital. But using a similar system could also have averted many other disasters, where using wrong units has ended with producing bad computation results. If the unit is always there together with the amount, the possibility for these kinds of errors is very much diminished. You can also add your own index methods if you have some programming skills and your problem domain is not well served by the existing indexes. There is already a respectable set of index types included in the core PostgreSQL, as well as several others which are developed outside the core.

The latest index method which became officially included in PostgreSQL is **KNN** (**K Nearest Neighbor**)—a clever index, which can return K rows ordered by their distance from the desired search target. One use of KNN is in fuzzy text search, where this can be used for ranking full-text search results by how well they match the search terms. Before KNN, this kind of thing was done by querying all rows which matched even a little, and then sorting all these by the distance function and returning K top rows as the last step.

If done using KNN index, the index access can start returning the rows in the desired order; so a simple LIMIT k function will return you the K top matches.

The KNN index can also be used for real distances, for example answering the request "Give me the 10 nearest pizza places to central station."

As you see, index types are separate from the data types they index. As another example, the same **GIN** (**General Inverted Index**) can be used for full-text search (together with stemmers, thesauri, and other text processing stuff) as well as indexing elements of integer arrays.

On caching

Yet another place where server-side programming can be used is for caching values, which are expensive to compute. The basic pattern here is:

1. Check if the value is cached.
2. If not or the value is too old, compute and cache it.
3. Return the cached value.

For example, calculating sales for a company is the perfect item to cache. Perhaps, a large retail company has 1,000 stores with potentially millions of individual sales transactions per day. If the corporate headquarters is looking for sales trends, it is much more efficient if the daily sales numbers were precalculated at the store level instead of summing up millions of daily transactions.

If the value is simple, like looking up a user's information from a single table based on the user ID, you don't need to do anything. The value becomes cached in PostgreSQL's internal page cache, and all lookups to it are so fast that even on a very fast network most of the time spent doing the lookups are in the network, not in the actual lookup. In such a case, getting data from a PostgreSQL database is as fast as getting it from any other in-memory cache (like memcached) but without any extra overhead in managing the cache.

Another use-case of caching is implementing materialized views. These are views which are precomputed only when needed, not each time one selects from that view. Some SQL databases have materialized views as a separate database object, but in PostgreSQL you have to do it all yourself, using other database features for automating the whole process.

Wrap up – why program in the server?

The main advantages of doing most data manipulation code server-side are the following.

Performance

Doing the computation near data is almost always a performance win, as the latencies for getting the data are minimal. In a typical data-intensive computation, most of the time tends to be spent in getting the data. Therefore, making data access inside the computation faster is the best way to make the whole thing fast. On my laptop it takes 2.2 ms to query one random row from a 1,00,000 row database into the client, but it takes only 0.12 ms to get the data inside the database. This is 20 times faster and this is inside the same machine over Unix sockets. The difference can be bigger if there is a network connection between client and server.

A small real-word story:

A friend of mine was called to help a large company (I'm sure you all know it, though I can't tell you which one) to try to make its e-mail sending application faster. They had implemented their e-mail generation system with all the latest Java EE technologies, first getting the data from the database, passing the data around between services, and serializing and de-serializing it several times before finally doing XSLT transform on the data to produce the e-mail text. The end result being that it produced only a few hundred e-mails per second and they were falling behind with their responses.

When he rewrote the process to use a PL/Perl function inside the database to format the data and the query returned already fully-formatted e-mails, it suddenly started spewing out tens of thousands of e-mails per second, and they had to add a second copy of sent mail to actually be able to send them out.

Ease of maintenance

If all data manipulation code is in a database, either as database functions or views, the actual upgrade process becomes very easy. All that is needed is running a DDL script that redefines the functions and all the clients automatically use the new code with no downtime, and no complicated coordination between several frontend systems and teams.

Simple ways to tighten security

If all access for some possibly insecure servers goes through functions, the database user of these servers use can be granted only the access to the needed functions and nothing else. They can't see the table data or even the fact that these tables exist. So even if that server becomes compromised, all it can do is continue to call the same functions. Also, there is no possibility to steal passwords, e-mails, or other sensitive information by issuing its own queries like SELECT * FROM users; and getting all the data there is in the database.

And the most important thing, programming in server is fun!

Summary

Programming inside the database server is not always the first thing that comes to mind to many developers, but it's unique placement inside the application stack gives it some powerful advantages. Your application can be faster, more secure, and more maintainable by pushing your logic into the database. With server-side programming in PostgreSQL, you can:

- Secure your data using functions
- Audit access to your data using triggers
- Enrich your data using custom data types
- Analyze your data using custom operators

And this is just the very start of what you can do inside PostgreSQL. Throughout the rest of this book, you will learn about many other ways to write powerful applications by programming inside PostgreSQL.

2
Server Programming Environment

You have had a chance to get acquainted with the general idea of using PostgreSQL, but now we are going to answer the question of why anyone would choose PostgreSQL as a development platform. As much as I like to believe that it's an easy decision for everyone, it's not.

For starters, let's get rid of the optimistic idea that anyone chooses a database platform for technical reasons. Sure, we would all like to think that we are objective, and we base our decisions on a preponderance of the technical evidence. This preponderance of evidence then indicates which features are available and relevant to our application. We would then proceed to make a weighted choice in favor of the most advantageous platform, and use the balance of the evidence to create workarounds and alternatives where our choice falls short. The fact is, we don't really understand all of the requirements of the application until we are halfway through the development cycle. Here are some reasons why:

- We don't know how the application will evolve over time. Many start-ups pivot from their initial idea as the market tells them to change.

- We don't know how many users there will *really* be until we have some registrations and can begin to measure the curve.

- We don't realize how important a particular feature could be until we get user feedback. The truth is that we don't really know much of the long term needs of the application until we're writing Version 2 or maybe even 3.

That is, unless you're one of the fortunate few that has a Research and Development department that writes the alpha version, throws it out the window, and then asks you to write the next version based on the lessons learned. Even then, you really don't know what the usage patterns are going to be once the application is deployed.

What we generally see in the PostgreSQL community, when new users start asking questions, are not people looking to make a decision, but rather people who already made a decision. In most cases, they are looking for technical justification for an existing plan of action. The decision point has already been passed. What I am going to write about in this chapter is not a TPC benchmark, nor is it about relative merits of PostgreSQL functions versus stored procedures. Frankly, nobody really cares about those things until after they have already made a choice and are trying to justify it.

This chapter contains the guide that I wish someone had written for me when I chose PostgreSQL back in 1998.

Cost of acquisition

One of biggest factors in deciding what technology is used in the application stack is the cost of acquisition. I've seen many application architectures drawn on a whiteboard where the technical team was embarrassed to show me, but they justified the design by trying to keep software licensing costs down. When it comes to the database environment, the usual suspects are Oracle, SQL Server, MySQL, and PostgreSQL. Oracle, the dominant player in the database space, is also the most costly. At the low end, Oracle does have reasonably priced offering and even a free express edition, but they are limited. Most people have needs beyond the low priced offerings and fall into the enterprise sales machine of Oracle. This usually results in a high price quote that makes your CFO fall out of his chair and you're back to designing your solution to keep your licensing costs down.

Then comes Microsoft SQL Server. This is your first reasonably viable option. The pricing is listed on the Microsoft website. I will not reproduce it here because the pricing schedule is too volatile for a book that will remain in print for more than 5 minutes. Nonetheless, an experienced thumb value of the purchase cost for SQL Server will get you running with a web capable model for about $5,000. This does not include a service contract. In the grand scheme of development costs, this is reasonable, and not too high of a barrier to enter.

Then we have the open source offerings, which are MySQL and PostgreSQL. They cost nothing, and the service contracts cost—wait for it—nothing. That is a very hard cost of acquisition to beat.

Remember in the beginning of the chapter, when I was talking about all of the things that you don't know when the project starts? Here's where the real win comes in. You can afford to fail.

There, I said it!

Low cost of acquisition is a synonym for *low cost of failure*. When we add up all of the unknowns for the project, we find out that we have a fairly good chance that the first iteration will not meet the market needs, and we need to have a way to jettison it quickly without long term contracts and additional costs of spinning up a new project.

This allows the project manager to move on to the next version using lessons learned from the consumer after the first version. Hopefully, this lesson in user acceptance will come at a very low cost, and the project will then begin to thrive the following version of this is bold (so are the versions on page 7) and begins a new paragraph - these should be consistent don't hang the success of the project on getting the first version perfect. You won't.

Availability of developers

This has been one of the most hilariously fun parts of my development life. I recently recommended using PostgreSQL for a reporting system in a local company. The company in question wanted to know if they chose PostgreSQL, would anyone on staff be able to maintain it. So I began to interview the developers to find out about their experience with PostgreSQL.

Me: Do you have any experience with PostgreSQL?

Developer 1: Yes, I used it at the last job for a product fulfillment project, but I don't think very many people have that experience. We should probably stick with MySQL.

Me: Do you have any experience with PostgreSQL?

Developer 2: Yes, I used it at the last job for a reporting project, but I don't think very many people have that experience. We should probably stick with MySQL.

After interviewing all seven developers that were influential on the project, I found that the only person without hands-on experience with PostgreSQL was the project manager. Since the project manager didn't expect to have any technical involvement in the project, he approved the selection of PostgreSQL.

PostgreSQL is one of the dirty little secrets of web developers. They have about the same level of familiarity with it as they do with encryption and security. Because "only advanced users" would use it, they have a general geek requirement to look into it, and presume that everyone else is too "inexperienced" to do the same. Everyone is trying to "dumb it down" for the other guy. They consider their own use of the tools at hand, (MySQL) a sacrifice that they are willing to make to help the less experienced fellow down the hall. Comically, the fellow down the hall thinks that he's making the same sacrifice for everyone else.

Lesson learned: Quit making choices for the "other guy". He is just as experienced (and intelligent) as you are, or might just want the opportunity to advance his skills.

Licensing

About two months after Oracle bought MySQL, they announced a plan that divided the development into two camps. There would now be a MySQL community edition and a professional version. The community edition would no longer gain any new features, and the professional version would become a commercial product.

There was a vast and thunderous sucking sound in the open source community, as they thrashed wildly about to find a new platform for Free and Open Source (FOSS) development.

Oracle immediately (in about 2 weeks) countermanded the order, and declared that things would stay as they were for the indefinite future. Those with short memories, forgiving hearts, or who just weren't paying attention went on about their business. Many other open source projects either switched to PostgreSQL or suddenly grew PostgreSQL database support.

Today we have MySQL and MySQL Enterprise Edition. If you want "backup, high availability, enterprise scalability, and the MySQL Enterprise monitor", you now have to pony up some dough. Capitalism is fine, and corporations have a right to charge money for their services and products in order to exist. But why should you as a project manager or developer have to pay for something that you can get for free?

Licensing is all about continued product availability and distribution. The PostgreSQL licensing model specifically states that you can have the source code, do anything with it that you want, redistribute it however you jolly well please, and those rights extend indefinitely. Try to get that deal with a commercial vendor.

As a corporate developer, PostgreSQL wins the legal battle for risk management hands down. I have heard the argument "I want to go with a commercial vendor in case I need someone to sue." I would encourage anyone who considers that a good argument to do a little research about how often these vendors have been sued, how often those suits were successful, and what the cost of court was for that success. I think you'll find that the only viable option is not to have that battle.

Predictability

This section could just as well have been titled "standards compliance," but I decided against it because the benefits of standards compliance in corporate projects are not obvious. The limitations of the common databases are well documented, and I will show you a few websites in a moment where you can make a comparison of who has the most "unintended behavior". I encourage you to read the material while thinking to yourself about the question, "Which method of feature development is most likely to make my application break in the future?"

```
http://www.sql-info.de/postgresql/postgres-gotchas.html
```

```
http://www.sql-info.de/mysql/gotchas.html
```

Spoiler alert: Stricter adherence to standards comes at the cost of not allowing ambiguous behavior. Not allowing ambiguous behavior makes the developer's life more difficult. Making the developer's life more difficult ensures that the interpretation of the commands that the developer gives will not change later, breaking the application.

Just how lazy can you afford to be? I'm not sure how to measure it. PostgreSQL is available for no cost future predictability, so I don't have to answer the question.

Sure, PostgreSQL also has some bugs listed. However, changes to the database core have a tendency to make the engine work like the documentation says it does, not like the documentation should have said. The PostgreSQL developers don't have to say "oops, I didn't think of that", very often. And when they do, PostgreSQL just becomes more standards compliant.

Community

Oracle and SQL Server don't have a community. Please understand when I say that, I mean that the chance that you will get to talk to a developer of the core database is about the same as your chance of winning the lottery. By the time you do, it's probably because you found a bug so heinous that it couldn't be ignored, and the only person who can understand your report is the guy that wrote the code in question. They have paid technical support, and that support has proven in my experience to be generally competent, but not stellar. I have had to work around the problem that I originally requested help with about 40 percent of the time.

Contrast that to MySQL and PostgreSQL, where just about anybody can speak to just about anybody else all day long. Many of the core developers of both the platforms can be found on IRC, met at conventions, contacted for contract development work, and for the most part, bribed remarkably easily with beer (hint, hint, wink, wink, nudge, nudge).

They are actively concerned with the health of the overall community, and will answer just about any kind of question you can ask. Even if the question has a very tenuous relationship to database development. My personal experience is that the PostgreSQL team has more core developers readily available more often than MySQL. They are also more personally available at conventions and meetings.

Did I mention they like beer?

Procedural languages

SQL Server allows you to create DLLs in any language that produces CLR. These DLLs must be loaded into the server at boot time. To create a procedure at run time and have it be immediately available, the only choice is the built in SQL dialect, Transact SQL (TSQL).

MySQL has a feature called **plugins**. One of the legal plugin types is a procedural language. Several languages have been tooled to work with MySQL via the plugin system, including most of the popular ones such as PHP and Python. These functions cannot be used for stored procedures or triggers, but they can be invoked from the common SQL statements. For the rest, you are stuck with the built-in SQL.

PostgreSQL has full support for additional procedural languages, which can be used to create any legal entity in the database that can be created with PL/pgSQL. The language can be added (or removed) from a running version of PostgreSQL and any function defined using that language may also be created or dropped while PostgreSQL is running. These languages have full access to PostgreSQL internal functions and all data entities that the calling user has permission.

There are many of these plugin language extensions available for PostgreSQL. I have used the ones for PHP, Python, bash, and PL/pgSQL. Yes, that means that the standard language for PostgreSQL is also installed and managed using the same extension system as any other language.

This brings us to the point that we have more developers available for PostgreSQL than you might have originally thought. Software developers are not required to learn a new development language to write stored procedures. They can extend PostgreSQL with the language of choice, and continue to code in the manner and workflow that they choose.

Lesson learned: There are no second class citizens in the PostgreSQL development community. Anyone can code in (almost) any language they choose.

Third-party tools: A frequent comparison point among the database platforms is the number of third-party applications available. I'm not so sure that the total number of them matters as much as the existence of applications you actually need.

To that end, following is a list of the products that I have used extensively with PostgreSQL:

- **Pentaho Data Integration (kettle)**: This is an outstanding **Extract Transform and Load (ETL)** tool
- **Pentaho Report Server**: This is a great reporting engine
- **PgAdmin3**: This is an awesome database administration tool
- **php5-postgesql**: This is a package to allow native access to PostgreSQL from PHP
- **Qcubed**: This is the PHP development framework with PostgreSQL support
- **Yii**: This is another great PHP development framework
- **Talend**: This is another ETL tool that works, but was not my favorite
- **BIRT**: This is a great JAVA reporting tool with easy report creation environment
- **psycopg2**: This is the Python bindings for PostgreSQL

These tools have made the PostgreSQL development experience a breeze and is no where near a complete list. We could fill this book with just a list of applications that support PostgreSQL and thanks to its liberal license, PostgreSQL is embedded in many commercial applications and you never really know it.

Lesson learned: Don't worry too much about how many tools are out there for the product. The ones that matter are available.

Platform compatibility

SQL Server is a Microsoft product. As such, it was and will always be a Microsoft platform tool. It is accessible to some limited degree via ODBC, but is not a serious choice for cross-platform development.

MySQL and PostgreSQL support every operating system currently available today. This ability (or lack of limitation) is a strong argument for long term stability. If any particular operating system is no longer available, or no longer supports open source software, it is fairly trivial to move the database server to another platform.

Lesson learned: In the commercial operating system wars, just say no.

Application design

> *"The thing that hath been, it is that which shall be; and that which is done is that which shall be done: and there is no new thing under the sun."*

> — *Ecclesiastes 1:8-10 KJV*

> *"... old things are passed away; behold, all things are become new."*

> — *2 Corinthians 5:16-18 KJV*

In software development, we are always running into the situation where what is old is new again and those developers who embrace a philosophy swear by it like a religion. We swing back and forth from thin server to thin client, between flat and hierarchical storage, from desktop application to web application and, most appropriately for this chapter, between client and server programming.

The reason for this swing between programming implementations has nothing to do with the features that the client or the server offers. Developer experience is a much more likely influence, and this influence can go in either direction, depending on what the developer encountered first.

I encourage both the server-centric developer and the client-centric developer to lay down their pitchforks while reading the rest of this chapter.

We will discuss, in due time, most of the new features of "server programming". If you're still not convinced by then, we will look at how you can harness the benefit of most of those features without leaving your application-centered point of view.

Databases are considered harmful

The simplest and least powerful way of looking at server programming is to view the database as a data bucket. Using only the most basic SQL statements of INSERT, SELECT, UPDATE, and DELETE, you can manipulate data a single row at a time and create application libraries for multiple databases very easily.

This approach has some major drawbacks. Moving data back and forth to the database server one row at a time is extremely inefficient and you will find that this method is simply not viable in a web scale application.

This idea is usually associated with a concept of a "data abstraction layer", a client library that allows the developer to switch the database out from under the application with very little effort. This abstraction layer is very useful in the open source development community, which allows the use of many databases, but they have no financial incentive to get the best possible performance.

In a 27 year career, I have never actually changed the database of an installed application without throwing away the application. One of the principles of agile software development is YAGNI (you ain't gonna need it). This is one of those cases.

Lesson learned: Data abstraction is valuable for projects that need to select a database platform at installation time. For everybody else, just say no.

Encapsulation

Another technique used in more client centric development philosophies is to try to isolate the database specific calls into a library of procedures. This design is usually aimed at leaving the application in control of all business logic. The application is still king, and the database is still just a necessary evil.

This view of database architecture sells the application developer short by ignoring a toolbox full of tools and choosing only the hammer. Everything in the application is then painted to look like a nail, and smacked with the hammer.

Lesson learned: Don't give up the power of the database just because it is not familiar. Use procedural languages and check out extension toolkits. There are some awesome pieces of work in there.

What does PostgreSQL offer?

So far we've mentioned procedural languages, functions, triggers, custom data types, and operators. These things can be created directly in the database via CREATE commands, or added as libraries using extensions.

Now we will show you some things you need to keep in mind when programming on the server in PostgreSQL.

Data locality

If at all possible, keep the data on the server. Believe me, it's happier there, and performance is much better when modifying data. If everything was done in the application layer, the data would need to be returned from the database, the modifications made, and then finally sent back to the database for a commit. If you are building a web-scalable application, this should be your last resort.

Let's walk through a small snippet using two methods of making an update to a single record:

```php
<?php
  $db = pg_connect("host port user password dbname schema");
  $sql = "SELECT * FROM customer WHERE id = 23";
  $row = pg_fetch_array($db,$sql);
  if ($row['account_balance'] > 6000) {
  $sql = "UPDATE customer SET valued_customer = true;";
  pg_query($db,$sql);
  }
  pg_close($db);
?>
```

This code snippet pulls a row of data from the database server to the client, makes an evaluation, and changes a customer account based on the evaluation. The result of the change is then sent back to the server for processing.

There are several things wrong with this scenario. First, the scalability is terrible. Imagine if this operation needed to be performed for thousands or even millions of customers.

The second problem is transactional integrity. What happens if the user's account balance changes from some other transaction between the query and the update? Is the customer still valued? That would depend on the business reason for the evaluation.

Try the following example:

```php
<?php
  $db = pg_connect('...');
  pg_query('UPDATE customer SET valued_customer = true WHERE balance > 6000;', $db);
  pg_close($db);
?>
```

This is simpler, has transactional integrity, and works for an incredibly large number of customers. Why point out such a simple and obvious example? Because many development frameworks work the "wrong" way by default. The code generator will produce some equivalent form of this example in the interest of being cross-platform, predictable, and easy to integrate into a simple design model.

This method promotes terrible practices. For systems that have a very low number of concurrent transactions, you will probably see what you would expect, but as concurrency increases, the number of unintended behaviors also increases.

The second example exposes a better philosophy: operate on columns, not rows, leave the data on the server, and let the database do the transactional work for you. That's what the database was made for.

More basics

It helps to have some basic background information before starting to program for the server. In the next few sections, we will explore the general technical environment in which you will be working. We will cover a lot of information, but don't worry too much about remembering it all right now. Just try to pick up the general idea.

Transactions

The default transaction isolation level in PostgreSQL is called **Read Committed**. This means that if multiple transactions attempt to modify the same data, they must wait for each other to finish before acting upon the resulting data. They wait in a first-come-first-served order. The final result of the data is what most people would naturally expect, reflecting the last chronological change.

PostgreSQL does not provide any way to do a dirty read. A dirty read is the ability to view the data the way it appears in someone else's transaction, and use it as if it were committed. This ability is not available in PostgreSQL because of the way that the multi-version concurrency control works.

There are other transaction isolation methods available, you can read about them in depth at http://www.postgresql.org/docs/9.2/static/transaction-iso.html.

It is important to note that when no transaction blocks are specified (BEGIN .. END), that PostgreSQL will treat each individual statement like a private transaction, and commit immediately when the statement is finished. This gives other transactions a chance to settle in between your statements. Some programming languages provide a transaction block around your statements, while some do not. Please check your language documentation to find out if you are running in a transacted session.

When using the two main clients to interact with PostgreSQL, the transaction behavior is different. The psql command line client does not provide transaction blocks for you. You are expected to know when to start/stop a transaction on your own. The **pgAdmin3** query window on the other hand wraps any statement that you submit into a transaction block for you. This is the way that it provides a cancel option. If the transaction is interrupted, a ROLLBACK will be performed and the database will go back to it's former state.

Some operations are exempt from transactions. For example, a sequence object will continue to increment even if the transaction fails and is rolled back. CREATE INDEX CONCURRENTLY requires management of it's own transactions, and should not be called from within a transaction block. The same is true with VACUUM as well as CLUSTER.

General error reporting and error handling

If you want to provide status to the user during your execution, you will become familiar with the commands RAISE, NOTICE, and NOTIFY. From a transactional perspective, the difference is that RAISE NOTICE will send the message immediately, even when wrapped in a transaction, while NOTIFY will wait for the transaction to settle before sending a message. NOTIFY will therefore not actually notify you of anything if the transaction fails and rolled back.

User-defined functions (UDF)

The ability to write user-defined functions is the powerhouse feature of PostgreSQL. Functions can be written in many different programming languages, use any kind of control structures that the language provides, and in the case of "untrusted" languages, can perform any operation that is available in PostgreSQL.

Functions can provide features that are not even directly SQL related. Some of the upcoming examples will show how to get network address information, query the system, move files around, and just about anything your heart desires.

So, how do we access this sugary goodness of PostgreSQL? We start by declaring that we want a function:

```
CREATE OR REPLACE FUNCTION addition (integer, integer) RETURNS integer
AS $$
DECLARE retval integer;
BEGIN
  SELECT $1 + $2 INTO retval;
  RETURN retval;
END;
$$ LANGUAGE plpgsql;
```

But what if we wanted to add three integers together?

```
CREATE OR REPLACE FUNCTION addition (integer, integer, integer)
RETURNS integer
AS $$
DECLARE retval integer;
BEGIN
  SELECT $1 + $2 +$3 INTO retval;
  RETURN retval;
END;
$$ LANGUAGE plpgsql;
```

We just invoked a concept called function overloading. This feature allows us to declare a function of the same name but with different parameters that potentially behave differently. This difference can be as subtle as just changing the data type of one of the arguments to the function. The function that PostgreSQL invokes depends on the closest match to the function arguments and expected return type.

But suppose we want to add together any number of integers? Well, PostgreSQL has a way to do that also.

```
CREATE OR REPLACE FUNCTION addition (VARIADIC arr integer[]) RETURNS
integer
AS $$
DECLARE retval integer;
BEGIN
    SELECT sum($1[i]) INTO retval FROM generate_subscripts($1, 1) g(i)
;
    RETURN retval;
END;
$$
LANGUAGE plpgsql;
```

This will allow us to pass in any number of integers, and get an appropriate response. These functions of course do not handle real or numeric data types. To handle other data types, simply declare the function again with those types, and call them with the appropriate parameters.

For more information about variable parameters, see http://www.postgresql.org/docs/9.2/static/xfunc-sql.html#XFUNC-SQL-VARIADIC-FUNCTIONS.

Other parameters

There is more than one way to get data into and out of a function. We can also declare IN/OUT parameters, return a table, return a set of records, and use cursors for both input and output.

This brings us to a special data type called ANY. It allows the parameter type to be undefined, and will allow any basic data type to be passed to the function. It is then up to the function to decide what to do with the data from there.

More control

Once you have your function written the way you need, PostgreSQL gives you additional control over how the function executes. You can control what data the function can access and how PostgreSQL will interpret the expense of running the function.

There are two statements that provide a security context for your functions. The first one is **Security Invoker**, which is the default security context. In the default context, the privileges of the calling user are respected by the function.

The other context is **Security Definer**. In this context, the user privileges of the creator of the function are respected during the execution of the function. Generally, this is used to temporarily escalate user rights for a specific purpose.

Cost can also be defined for the function. This cost will help the query planner estimate how expensive it is to call your function. Higher orders of cost will cause the query planner to change the access path so your function will be called as few times as possible. The PostgreSQL documentation shows these numbers to be a factor of cpu_operator_cost. That's more than a little misleading. The numbers have no direct correlation to CPU cycles. They are only relevant in comparison with one another. It's more like how some national money compares with the rest of the European Union. Some Euros are more equal than others.

To estimate your own function's complexity, start with the language you are implementing it in. For C, the default would be 1 * number of records returned. For Python, 1.5. For scripting languages such as PHP, a more appropriate number might be 100. For plsh, you might want to use 150 or more depending on how many external tool calls are involved in getting an answer. The default is 100, and that seems to work reasonably well for PL/pgSQL.

Summary

Now you know a few things about the PostgreSQL environment, as well as some things that will help you in the unforeseeable future. PostgreSQL is built to handle your needs, but more importantly, it is built *not* to change underneath you in the future.

We touched a little on the environment and called out some of the more important things to keep in mind while programming on the server in PostgreSQL. Don't worry too much if you don't remember all of it. It is fine to go on to the next chapter, where we actually start making some useful functions. Then come back and review this chapter when you have a clearer understanding of the features available to the function writer.

Your First PL/pgSQL Function

3

A function is the basic building block for extending PostgreSQL. A function accepts input in the form of parameters, and can create output in the form of output parameters or return values. Many functions are provided by PostgreSQL itself such as the common mathematical functions, for example, square root and absolute value. For a comprehensive list of what is already available, go to http://www.postgresql.org/docs/current/static/functions.html.

The functions that you create have all of the same privileges and power that the built-in functions possess. The developers of PostgreSQL use the same libraries to extend the database that you use as a developer to write your business logic.

This means that you have the tools available to be a first class citizen of the PostgreSQL development community. In fact, there are no second-class seats on this bus.

A function accepts parameters that can be of any data type available in PostgreSQL and it returns results to the caller using any of the same types. What you do within the function is entirely up to you. You have been enabled to do anything that PostgreSQL is capable of doing. You are herewith also warned that you are capable of doing anything that PostgreSQL is capable of doing. The training wheels are off.

In this chapter, you will learn:

- The basic building blocks of a PostgreSQL function
- Passing parameters into a function
- Basic control structures inside of a function
- Returning results out of a function

Why PL/pgSQL?

PL/pgSQL is a powerful SQL scripting language heavily influenced by PL/SQL, the stored procedure language distributed with Oracle. It is included in the vast majority of PostgreSQL installations as a standard part of the product, so it usually requires no setup at all to begin.

PL/pgSQL also has a dirty little secret. The PostgreSQL developers don't want you to know that it is a full-fledged SQL development language, capable of doing pretty much anything within the PostgreSQL database.

Why is that a secret? For years, PostgreSQL did not claim to have stored procedures. PL/pgSQL functions were originally designed to return scalar values and were intended for simple mathematical tasks and trivial string manipulation.

Over the years, PL/pgSQL grew a rich set of control structures and gained the ability to be used by triggers, operators, and indexes. In the end, the developers were grudgingly forced to admit that they had a complete stored procedure development system on their hands.

Along the way, the goal of PL/pgSQL changed from simplistic scalar functions to providing access to all of the PostgreSQL system internals with full control structure. The full list of what is available in the current version is provided at `http://www.postgresql.org/docs/current/static/plpgsql-overview.html`.

Today, some of the benefits of using PL/pgSQL are:

- It is easy to use
- It is available by default on most deployments of PostgreSQL
- It is optimized for performance of data intensive tasks

In addition to PL/pgSQL, PostgreSQL also allows many other languages to be plugged in to the database, some of which we will cover in this book. You may also choose to write your functions in Perl, Python, PHP, bash, and a host of other languages, but they will likely need to be added to your instance of PostgreSQL.

Structure of a PL/pgSQL function

It doesn't take much to get a PL/pgSQL function working. Here is a very basic example:

```
CREATE FUNCTION mid(varchar, integer, integer) RETURNS varchar
AS $$
BEGIN
  RETURN substring($1,$2,$3);
```

```
END;
$$
LANGUAGE plpgsql;
```

The previous function shows the minimal elements of a PL/pgSQL function. It creates an alias for the substring built-in function called mid. This is a handy alias to have around for developers that come from Microsoft SQL Server or MySQL and are wondering what happened to the mid function. It also illustrates the most basic parameter passing strategy. The parameters are not named and are accessed in the function by relative location from left to right.

The basic elements are name, parameters, return type, body, and language. It could be argued that parameters are not mandatory for a function and neither is the return value. This might be useful for a procedure that operates on data without providing a response, but it would be prudent to return a value of TRUE to indicate that the procedure succeeded.

Accessing function arguments

Function arguments can also be passed and accessed by name, instead of just by the ordinal order. By accessing the parameters by name, it makes the resulting function code a little more readable. The following is an example of a function that uses named parameters:

```
CREATE FUNCTION mid(keyfield varchar, starting_point integer)
  RETURNS varchar
AS
$$
BEGIN
  RETURN substring(keyfield,starting_point);
END
$$
LANGUAGE plpgsql;
```

The previous function also demonstrates overloading of the mid function. Overloading is another feature of PostgreSQL functions, which allows for multiple procedures using the same name, but different parameters. In this case, we first declared the mid function with three parameters, but in this example, overloading is used to implement an alternative form of the mid function where there are only two parameters. When the third parameter is omitted, the result will be the string starting from starting_point and continuing to the end of the input string.

```
SELECT mid('Kirk L. Roybal',9);
```

The previous line of code yields the following result:

```
Roybal
```

In order to access the function parameters by name, PostgreSQL makes a few educated guesses depending on the statement. Consider for a moment the following function:

```
CREATE OR REPLACE FUNCTION ambiguous(parameter varchar) RETURNS
   integer  AS $$
DECLARE retval integer;
BEGIN

INSERT INTO parameter (parameter) VALUES (parameter) RETURNING id
   INTO retval;
RETURN retval;

END
$$
language plpgsql;

SELECT ambiguous ('parameter');
```

This is an example of positively atrocious programming that should never occur outside of an example of how *not* to write functions. However, PostgreSQL is intelligent enough to correctly deduce that the contents of the function parameter are only legal in the VALUES list. All other occurrences of "parameter" are actually physical PostgreSQL entities.

We also introduced an optional section to the function. We declare a variable before the BEGIN statement. Variables that appear in this section are valid during the execution of the function.

Also of note in this function is the RETURNING id INTO retval statement. This feature allows the developer to specify the identity field of the record, and return the value of that field after the record has been inserted. Our function then returns this value to the caller as an indicator that the function succeeded and a way to find the record that has been inserted.

Conditional expressions

Conditional expressions allow developers to control the action of the function based on a defined criteria. The following is an example of using a CASE statement to control how a string is treated based on its value. If the value is null, or contains a zero length string, it is treated the same as null.

```
CREATE OR REPLACE FUNCTION format_us_full_name(

                            prefix text, firstname text,

                            mi text, lastname text,

                            suffix text)

  RETURNS text AS

$$

DECLARE

   fname_mi text;

   fmi_lname text;

   prefix_fmil text;

   pfmil_suffix text;

BEGIN

   fname_mi := CONCAT_WS(' ',

                            CASE trim(firstname)

                               WHEN ''

                               THEN NULL

                               ELSE firstname

                            END,

                            CASE trim(mi)
```

```
                                          WHEN ''

                                          THEN NULL

                                          ELSE mi

                                        END || '.');
        fmi_lname := CONCAT_WS(' ',

                                      CASE fname_mi

                                        WHEN ''

                                        THEN NULL

                                        ELSE fname_mi

                                      END,

                                      CASE trim(lastname)

                                        WHEN ''

                                        THEN NULL

                                        ELSE lastname

                                      END);

        prefix_fmil := CONCAT_WS('. ',

                                        CASE trim(prefix)

                                          WHEN ''

                                          THEN NULL

                                          ELSE prefix

                                        END,

                                        CASE fmi_lname

                                          WHEN ''
```

```
                                        THEN NULL

                                        ELSE fmi_lname

                                    END);

    pfmil_suffix := CONCAT_WS(', ',

                                        CASE prefix_fmil

                                          WHEN ''

                                          THEN NULL

                                          ELSE prefix_fmil

                                        END,

                                        CASE trim(suffix)

                                          WHEN ''

                                          THEN NULL

                                          ELSE suffix || '.'

                                    END);


    RETURN pfmil_suffix;

END;

$$

    LANGUAGE plpgsql;
```

The idea here is that when any element of a full name is missing, the surrounding punctuation and white space should also be missing. This function returns a well formatted full name of a person in the USA, with as much of the name filled in as possible. When running this function, you will see the following:

```
postgres=# select format_us_full_name('Mr', 'Martin', 'L', 'King',
   'Jr');

   format_us_full_name
```

```
--------------------------

 Mr. Martin L. King, Jr.

(1 row)



postgres=# select format_us_full_name('', 'Martin', 'L', 'King',
  'Jr');

 format_us_full_name

----------------------

 Martin L. King, Jr.

(1 row)
```

Another way to use conditional expressions is by using the IF/THEN/ELSE blocks. The following is the same function again written using IF statements rather than CASE statements:

```
CREATE OR REPLACE FUNCTION format_us_full_name(

                         prefix text, firstname text,

                         mi text, lastname text,

                         suffix text)

  RETURNS text AS

$$

DECLARE

  fname_mi text;

  fmi_lname text;

  prefix_fmil text;

  pfmil_suffix text;
```

```
BEGIN

    fname_mi := CONCAT_WS(' ',
                                IF(trim(firstname)
                                  ='',NULL,firstname),

                                IF(trim(mi) = '', NULL, mi ||
                                  '.')
                          );

    fmi_lname := CONCAT_WS(' ',
                                IF(fname_mi = '',NULL,
                                  fname_mi),

                                IF(trim(lastname) =  '', NULL,
                                  lastname)
                          );

    prefix_fmil := CONCAT_WS('. ',
                                    IF(trim(prefix) = '', NULL,
                                      prefix),

                                    IF(fmi_lname = '', NULL,
                                      fmi_lname)
                          );

    pfmil_suffix := CONCAT_WS(', ',
                                     IF (prefix_fmil = '', NULL,
                                       prefix_fmil),

                                     IF (trim(suffix) = '',
                                       NULL, suffix || '.')
                              );


    RETURN pfmil_suffix;

END;

$$

    LANGUAGE plpgsql;
```

PostgreSQL PL/pgSQL provides several more syntactical variants of these conditional expressions. This introduction has focused on the most commonly used ones. For a more complete discussion of the topic, visit http://www.postgresql. org/docs/current/static/functions-conditional.html.

Loops with counters

The PL/pgSQL language provides a simple way to loop through some elements. The following is a function that returns the *n*th Fibonacci sequence number:

```
CREATE OR REPLACE FUNCTION fib(n integer)

  RETURNS decimal(1000,0)

AS $$

  DECLARE counter integer := 0;

  DECLARE a decimal(1000,0) := 0;

  DECLARE b decimal(1000,0) := 1;

BEGIN

  IF (n < 1) THEN

    RETURN 0;

  END IF;


  LOOP

    EXIT WHEN counter = n;

    counter := counter + 1;

    SELECT  b,a+b INTO a,b;

  END LOOP;
```

```
   RETURN a;

   END;

   $$

   LANGUAGE plpgsql;


   SELECT fib(4);
```

The previous code results in 3 as the output.

The highest Fibonacci number we can calculate with this function is 4785. If a value of the parameter is larger than that, the result will not fit into the 1000 length decimal we declared to return.

Just for the record, in the Fibonacci sequence each element in the sequence is the sum of the previous 2 elements. Thus, the first few elements of the sequence should be 0,1,1,2,3,5,8,13,21,34, and so on. There are a few PostgreSQL Fibonacci sequence functions out there on the interwebs, but they use the dreaded recursive method. In this case recursion is a Bad Thing™.

In this function, we also introduced default values to the variables in the declarations section. When the function is invoked, the variables will be initially set to these values.

Also take a quick gander at the statement SELECT b,a+b INTO a,b. This statement makes two variable assignments at the same time. It avoids the use of a third variable while acting on both a and b.

For some additional looping syntax, take a look at the PostgreSQL documentation page at http://www.postgresql.org/docs/current/static/plpgsql-control-structures.html.

Looping through query results

Before we embark on this journey through query result loops, I think it is fair to warn you that if you are using this method you are probably Doing It Wrong™. This is one of the most processor and memory intensive operations that PostgreSQL offers. There are exceedingly few reasons to iterate through a result set on the database server that offset this cost. I would encourage you to think very hard about how to implement the same idea using a function, values list in a query, temporary table, and permanent table, or precompute the values in any way possible to avoid this operation. So, do you still think you have an overwhelming reason to use this technique? Ok, read on.

The following is the simple version:

```
FOR row IN EXECUTE

     'SELECT * FROM job_queue q WHERE NOT processed LIMIT 100'

LOOP

    CASE q.process_type

     WHEN 'archive_point_of_sale'

       THEN   INSERT INTO hist_orders (...)

              SELECT ... FROM orders

                 INNER JOIN order_detail ...

                 INNER JOIN item ...;

     WHEN 'prune_archived_orders'

       THEN DELETE FROM order_detail

              WHERE order_id in (SELECT order_id FROM
                hist_orders);

              DELETE FROM orders

              WHERE order_id IN (SELECT order_id FROM
                hist_orders);

      ELSE

   RAISE NOTICE 'Unknown process_type: %', q.process_type;

     END;


     UPDATE job_queue SET processed = TRUE WHERE id = q.id;

END LOOP;
```

The previous example shows a basic strategy pattern of processing messages in a job queue. Using this technique, rows in a table contain a list of jobs that need to be processed.

We introduce the EXECUTE statement here, too. The SELECT statement is a string value. Using EXECUTE, we can dynamically build PL/pgSQL commands as strings and then invoke them as statements against the database. This technique comes in handy when we want to change the table name or other SQL keywords that make up our statement. These parts of the SQL statement cannot be stored in variables, and are not generally "changeable". With EXECUTE, we can change any part of the statement we jolly well please.

The following is an example that comes from the PostgreSQL documentation that shows dynamic commands running inside of a loop:

```
CREATE FUNCTION cs_refresh_mviews() RETURNS integer AS $$

DECLARE

    mviews RECORD;

BEGIN

    PERFORM cs_log('Refreshing materialized views...');



    FOR mviews IN SELECT * FROM cs_materialized_views ORDER BY
      sort_key LOOP



        -- Now "mviews" has one record from cs_materialized_views



        PERFORM cs_log('Refreshing materialized view ' ||
          quote_ident(mviews.mv_name) || ' ...');

        EXECUTE 'TRUNCATE TABLE ' || quote_ident(mviews.mv_name);

        EXECUTE 'INSERT INTO ' || quote_ident(mviews.mv_name) || '
          ' || mviews.mv_query;
```

```
        END LOOP;


        PERFORM cs_log('Done refreshing materialized views.');

        RETURN 1;

    END;

    $$ LANGUAGE plpgsql;
```

The previous looping example shows a more complex function that refreshes the data in some staging tables. These staging tables are designated "materialized views" because the data is actually physically transferred to the staging tables. This method is a common way to reduce query execution overhead for many presentations of the same data. In this case, the inefficiency of looping is trivial compared to the continued cost of repeated queries to the same data.

PERFORM versus SELECT

You may have noticed a statement in the previous example that we haven't covered yet. PERFORM is the command to use when you want to just discard the results of a statement. If the previous example were changed to:

```
    SELECT cs_log("Done refreshing materialized views");
```

The query engine would return No destination for result data.

We could retrieve the results into variables and then proceed to ignore the variables, but that is just a little too sloppy for my taste. By using the PERFORM statement, we have indicated that ignoring the results was not accidental. We were happy with the fact that the log was appended to blindly, and if it wasn't, oh well, we didn't fail to continue the execution because of a log entry issue.

Returning a record

All of our function examples so far have featured a simple scalar value in the RETURN clause. For more complex return types, we have several choices. One option is to return a set of records conforming to a table definition. For the sake of this example, we will assume that you are in the middle of a big software development upgrade procedure that uses a name/value pair table structure to store settings. You have been asked to change the table structure from the key and value columns to a series of columns where the column name is now the name of the key. By the way, you also need to preserve the settings for every version of the software you have ever deployed.

Looking at the existing CREATE TABLE statement for the table you have to work with, we find:

```
CREATE TABLE application_settings_old (
version varchar(200),
key varchar(200),
value varchar(2000));
```

When you run a select statement against the table, you find out that there are not very many settings, but there have been quite a few versions of them. So you make a new table that is a little more explicit.

```
CREATE TABLE  application_settings_new (
version varchar(200),
full_name varchar(2000),
description varchar(2000),
print_certificate varchar(2000),
show_advertisements varchar(2000),
show_splash_screen varchar(2000));
```

Transforming the settings data into this new format can be accomplished with an insert statement and a function that conveniently returns our data to us in the new table format.

Let's go ahead and define the function:

```
CREATE OR REPLACE FUNCTION

    flatten_application_settings(app_version varchar(200))

RETURNS setof application_settings_new

AS $$
```

```
BEGIN

    -- Create a temporary table to hold a single row of data

    IF EXISTS (SELECT relname FROM pg_class WHERE
      relname='tmp_settings')

    THEN

      TRUNCATE TABLE tmp_settings;

    ELSE

      CREATE TEMP TABLE tmp_settings (LIKE
        application_settings_new);

    END IF;



    -- the row will contain all of the data for this application
      version

    INSERT INTO tmp_settings (version) VALUES (app_version);



    -- add the details to the record for this application version

    UPDATE tmp_settings

    SET full_name = (SELECT value

                        FROM application_settings_old

                      WHERE version = app_version

                        AND key='full_name'),

        description = (SELECT value

                          FROM application_settings_old
```

```
                         WHERE version = app_version

                           AND key='description'),

      print_certificate = (SELECT value

                              FROM application_settings_old

                            WHERE version = app_version

                              AND key='print_certificate'),

      show_advertisements = (SELECT value

                                 FROM application_settings_old

                               WHERE version - app_version

                                 AND key='show_advertisements'),

      show_splash_screen = (SELECT value

                               FROM application_settings_old

                             WHERE version = app_version

                               AND key='show_splash_screen');



   -- hand back the results to the caller

   RETURN QUERY SELECT * FROM tmp_settings;



   END;

   $$ LANGUAGE plpgsql;
```

The previous function returns a single row of data to the calling query. The row contains all of the settings that were previously defined as key/value pairs, but now are explicitly defined fields. The function and the final table could also be enhanced to transform the data types of the settings to something more explicit. But hey, I'm just a lowly book author, not a "real" developer, so I'll leave that one up to you.

We then proceed to use the function to do the transformation:

```
INSERT INTO application_settings_new
SELECT ( flatten_application_settings(version)).*
FROM (
SELECT version
FROM application_settings_old
GROUP BY version)
```

And violá! The data is now available in tabular form in the new table structure.

Acting on function results

The previous example showed one way to retrieve and further process function results. The following are a few more useful ways to call a function:

```
SELECT fib(55);
SELECT (flatten_application_settings('9.08.97')).*
SELECT * FROM flatten_application_settings('9.08.97');
```

Any of the previous methods will create a legal field list in PostgreSQL, which in turn can be used in any way that fields in a simple SELECT statement on a table are used.

The example from the previous section used the results of the flatten_application_settings() function, a source of data for an INSERT statement. The following is an example of how to use the same function as a data source for UPDATE:

```
UPDATE application_settings_new

   SET full_name = flat.full_name,

       description  = flat.description,

       print_certificate = flat.print_certificate,

       show_advertisements = flat.show_advertisements,

       show_splash_screen = flat.show_splash_screen

  FROM flatten_application_settings('9.08.97') flat;
```

Using the application version as a key, we can update the records in the new table. Isn't that a really handy way to keep up with changes to the application settings, while both the old and new applications are still active? I'll take any compliments in the form of cash (or beer), please.

Summary

Writing functions in PostgreSQL is an extremely powerful tool. PostgreSQL functions provide the ability to add functionality to the database core to increase performance, security, and maintainability.

They can be written in just about any language that is available to the open source community, and several that are proprietary. If the language that you would like to write them in is not available, it can be made available quickly and easily through a very robust and complete compatibility layer.

4
Returning Structured Data

In the previous chapter, we have seen functions that return single values. They returned either a "scalar", simple types such as integer, text, or data, or a more complex type similar to a row in the database table. In this chapter, we will expand these concepts and show how you can return your data to the client in much more powerful ways.

In this chapter, we will examine multiple rows of both scalar types, as well as learn about several ways of defining complex types for function return values.

We will also examine differences between SETOF scalars, or rows and arrays of the same. Later, we will also examine returning CURSORs, which are kind of "lazy" tables, that is something that can be used to get a set of rows but may not yet have actually evaluated or fetched the rows. As the modern world is not about rigidly table-structured data, we will also examine ways of dealing with more complex data structures, both predefined and dynamically created.

But let's start from a simple example and then add more features and variants as we go.

Sets and arrays

Rowsets are very similar to arrays in many ways, but they mainly differ in how you can use them. For most data manipulations, you want to use rowsets, as the SQL language is designed to deal with them. Arrays, however, are most useful for static storage. They are more complicated for client applications to use than rowsets, with usability features missing such as no simple and straightforward built-in way to iterate over them.

Returning sets

When you write a set returning function, there are some differences from a normal scalar function. Let's first take a look at returning a set of integers.

Returning a set of integers

We will revisit our Fibonacci number generating function, but this time we will not return just the *n*th number, but the whole sequence of numbers up to the *n*th number.

```
CREATE OR REPLACE FUNCTION fibonacci_seq(num integer)
  RETURNS SETOF integer AS $$
DECLARE
  a int := 0;
  b int := 1;
BEGIN
  IF (num <= 0)
    THEN RETURN;
  END IF;

  RETURN NEXT a;
  LOOP
    EXIT WHEN num <= 1;
    RETURN NEXT b;

      num = num - 1;
      SELECT b, a + b INTO a, b;
  END LOOP;
END;
$$ language plpgsql;
```

The first difference we see is that instead of returning a single integer value, this function is defined as returning a SETOF integer.

Then if you examine the code carefully, you see that there are two different types of RETURN statements. First is the ordinary RETURN function in the following code snippet:

```
IF (num <= 0)
    THEN RETURN;
```

In this case it is used to terminate the function early if the length of desired sequence of Fibonacci numbers is zero or less.

The second kind of RETURN statement is used to return values and continue execution:

```
RETURN NEXT a;
```

You may have noticed that there are a few other things we did differently in this Fibonacci example than we did earlier. First, we declared and initialized the variables a and b inside the DECLARE section, instead of first declaring and then initializing them. We also used the argument as a down counter instead of using a separate variable for counting from zero and then comparing it with the argument.

Both of these techniques save a few lines of code and may make the code more readable depending on your preferences. But the longer versions might be easier to follow and understand, so we don't particularly endorse either way.

Using a set-returning function

A set-returning function (also known as a table function) can be used in most places a table, view, or subquery can be used. They are a powerful and flexible way to return your data.

You can call the function in the SELECT clause like you do with a scalar function:

```
postgres=# SELECT fibonacci_seq(3);
 fibonacci_seq
---------------
             0
             1
             1
(3 rows)
```

You can also call the function as part of the FROM clause:

```
postgres=# SELECT * FROM fibonacci_seq(3);
 fibonacci_seq
---------------
             0
             1
             1
(3 rows)
```

You can even call it in the WHERE clause:

```
postgres=# SELECT * FROM fibonacci_seq(3) WHERE 1 = ANY
  (SELECT fibonacci_seq(3));
 fibonacci_seq
---------------
```

```
                    0
                    1
                    1
      (3 rows)
```

Using database side functions for all data access is a great way to secure your application, help with performance, and allow for easy maintenance. Table functions allow you to use functions in all cases where you would have been forced to use more complex queries from the client if only scalar functions would have been available.

Returning rows from a function

It would often be very helpful to return back to the client even more information than a set of integers. You may need all of the columns from an existing table, and the simplest way to declare a return type for a function is to just use the table as part of the return definition.

```
CREATE OR REPLACE FUNCTION installed_languages()
  RETURNS SETOF pg_language AS $$
BEGIN
    RETURN QUERY SELECT * FROM  pg_language;
END;
$$ LANGUAGE plpgsql;
```

Notice that you still need the SETOF part, but instead of defining it as a set of integers, we use pg_language which is a table.

You could also have used TYPE defined using the CREATE TYPE command or even VIEW:

```
hannu=# select * from installed_languages();

-[ RECORD 1 ]-+----------
lanname       | internal
lanowner      | 10
lanispl       | f
lanpltrusted  | f
lanplcallfoid | 0
laninline     | 0
lanvalidator  | 2246
lanacl        |
-[ RECORD 2 ]-+----------
lanname       | c
lanowner      | 10
lanispl       | f
```

```
lanpltrusted  | f
lanplcallfoid | 0
laninline     | 0
lanvalidator  | 2247
lanacl        |
-[ RECORD 3 ]-+----------
lanname       | sql
lanowner      | 10
lanispl       | f
lanpltrusted  | t
lanplcallfoid | 0
laninline     | 0
lanvalidator  | 2248
lanacl        |
-[ RECORD 4 ]-+----------
lanname       | plpgsql
lanowner      | 10
lanispl       | t
lanpltrusted  | t
lanplcallfoid | 12596
laninline     | 12597
lanvalidator  | 12598
lanacl        |
-[ RECORD 5 ]-+----------
lanname       | plpythonu
lanowner      | 10
lanispl       | t
lanpltrusted  | f
lanplcallfoid | 17563
laninline     | 17564
lanvalidator  | 17565
lanacl        |
```

Functions based on views

Creating a function based on a view definition is a very powerful and flexible way of providing information to users. As an example of this, I will tell a story of how I started a simple utility view for answering the question, "What queries are running now and which ones have been running the longest time?" It evolved into a function based on this view plus a few more views based on the function.

The way to get all data to answer this question in PostgreSQL is by using the following query:

```
hannu=# select * from pg_stat_activity;

-[ RECORD 1 ]----+---------------------------------
datid            | 17557
datname          | hannu
pid              | 8933
usesysid         | 10
usename          | postgres
application_name | psql
client_addr      |
client_hostname  |
client_port      | -1
backend_start    | 2013-03-19 13:47:45.920902-04
xact_start       | 2013-03-19 14:05:47.91225-04
query_start      | 2013-03-19 14:05:47.91225-04
state_change     | 2013-03-19 14:05:47.912253-04
waiting          | f
state            | active
query            | select * from pg_stat_activity;
```

The usual process is to use a variant of the following query, here already wrapped into a view:

```
CREATE VIEW running_queries AS
SELECT
    CURRENT_TIMESTAMP - query_start as runtime,
    pid,
    usename,
    waiting,
    query
FROM pg_stat_activity
ORDER BY 1 DESC
LIMIT 10;
```

But soon you will notice, that putting this query into a view is not enough. Sometimes you want to vary the number of lowest queries, sometimes you don't want to have the full query text, but just the beginning, and so on.

If you want to vary some parameters, the logical thing is to use a function instead of a view, as follows:

```
CREATE OR REPLACE FUNCTION running_queries(rows int, qlen int)
  RETURNS SETOF running_queries AS
$$
BEGIN
   RETURN QUERY SELECT
      runtime,
      pid,
      usename,
      waiting,
      substring(query,1,qlen) as query
   FROM running_queries
   ORDER BY 1 DESC
   LIMIT rows;
END;
$$ LANGUAGE plpgsql;
```

As a security precaution, the default behavior of the `pg_stat_activity` view is that only superusers can see what other users are running. Sometimes it may be necessary to allow the non-superusers to see at least the type of query (`SELECT`, `INSERT`, `DELETE`, or `UPDATE`) other users are running, but hide the exact contents. To do so, you have to make two changes to the previous function.

First, replace the row for getting `current_query` with the following code snippet:

```
(CASE WHEN ( usename= session_user )
      OR (select usesuper
            from pg_user
            where usename = session_user)
     THEN
       substring(query,1,qlen)
     ELSE
       substring(ltrim(query), 1, 6) || ' ***'
     END  )as query
```

This code snippet checks each row to see if the user running the function has permission to see the full query. If the user is a superuser, then he has permission to see the full query. If the user is a regular user, he will only see the full query for his queries. All other rows will only show the first six characters followed by *** to mark it as a shortened query string.

The other key point to allowing ordinary users to run the function is to grant them the appropriate rights to do so. When a function is created, the default behavior is to run with Security Invoker rights, which means that the function will be called with the rights of the user who called it. To easily grant the correct rights to call the function, the function needs to be created with Security Definer privileges. This causes the function to execute with the privileges of the user that created the function, so creating the function as a superuser will allow it to execute as a superuser.

Now you have a function which you can use to get the start of the five longest running queries using the following query:

```
SELECT * FROM running_queries(5,25);
```

Or to get complete a query you can use:

```
SELECT * FROM running_queries(1000,1024);
```

You may want to define a few convenience views for the variants you use most.

```
CREATE OR REPLACE VIEW running_queries_tiny AS
SELECT * FROM running_queries(5,25);
CREATE VIEW running_queries_full AS
SELECT * FROM running_queries(1000,1024);
```

You may even redefine the original view to use the first version of the function.

```
CREATE OR REPLACE VIEW running_queries AS
SELECT * FROM running_queries(5,25);
```

This is usually not recommended, but it demonstrates three important things:

- Views and functions can have exactly the same name
- You can get a circular reference by basing a function on a view and then basing a view on that function
- If you get a circular reference this way, you can't easily change either definition

To resolve this, simply avoid circular references.

Even without circular references, there is still a dependency on the view called from the function. If, for instance, you need to add a column to show the application name to the running_queries view. The function needs to change as well.

```
CREATE OR REPLACE VIEW running_queries AS
SELECT
    CURRENT_TIMESTAMP - query_start as runtime,
    pid,
```

```
    usename,
    waiting,
    query,
    application_name as appname
FROM pg_stat_activity
ORDER BY 1 DESC
LIMIT 10;
```

The view definition can be changed without an error, but the next time you try to run the running_queries(int, int) function, you get an error.

```
hannu=# select * from running_queries(5,25);
ERROR:  structure of query does not match function result type
DETAIL:  Number of returned columns (5) does not match expected
  column count (6).
CONTEXT:  PL/pgSQL function "running_queries" line 3 at RETURN
  QUERY
```

To fix this, you need to add the additional column to the function.

```
CREATE OR REPLACE FUNCTION running_queries(rows int, qlen int)
  RETURNS SETOF running_queries AS
$$
BEGIN
   RETURN QUERY SELECT
      runtime,
      pid,
      usename,
      waiting,
    (CASE WHEN ( usename= session_user )
       OR (select usesuper
              from pg_user
             where usename = session_user)
       THEN
         substring(query,1,qlen)
       ELSE
         substring(ltrim(query), 1, 6) || ' ***'
       END) as query,
       appname
    FROM running_queries
   ORDER BY 1 DESC
   LIMIT rows;
END;
$$
LANGUAGE plpgsql
SECURITY DEFINER;
```

OUT parameters and records

Using a pre-existing type, table, or view for compound return types is a simple mechanism for returning more complex structures. However, there is often a need to define the return type of the function with the function itself and not be dependent on other objects. This is especially true when managing changes to a running application, so over time two better ways to handle this have been added to PostgreSQL.

OUT parameters

Up until this point, all of the functions we have created have used parameters that are defined as IN parameters. The IN parameters are meant to just pass information into the function that can be used, but not returned. Parameters can also be defined as OUT or INOUT parameters if you want the function to return some information as well.

```
CREATE OR REPLACE FUNCTION positives(
                    INOUT a int,
                    INOUT b int,
                    INOUT c int)
AS $$
BEGIN
    IF a < 0 THEN a = null; END IF;
    IF b < 0 THEN b = null; END IF;
    IF c < 0 THEN c = null; END IF;
END;
$$ LANGUAGE plpgsql;
```

When we run the previous function, notice that it only returns a single row of data.

```
hannu=# SELECT * FROM positives(-1, 1, 2);
-[ RECORD 1 ]
a |
b | 1
c | 2
```

Returning records

If multiple rows of data are needed to be returned, a similar function returning a set is achieved by adding RETURNS SETOF RECORD. This technique can only be used with functions using INOUT or OUT arguments.

```
CREATE FUNCTION permutations(INOUT a int,
                            INOUT b int,
                            INOUT c int)
```

```
RETURNS SETOF RECORD
AS $$
BEGIN
    RETURN NEXT;
    SELECT b,c INTO c,b; RETURN NEXT;
    SELECT a,b INTO b,a; RETURN NEXT;
    SELECT b,c INTO c,b; RETURN NEXT;
    SELECT a,b INTO b,a; RETURN NEXT;
    SELECT b,c INTO c,b; RETURN NEXT;
END;
$$ LANGUAGE plpgsql;
```

Running the `permutations` function returns the six rows we would expect:

```
hannu=# SELECT * FROM permutations(1, 2, 3);
-[ RECORD 1 ]
a | 1
b | 2
c | 3
-[ RECORD 2 ]
a | 1
b | 3
c | 2
-[ RECORD 3 ]
a | 3
b | 1
c | 2
-[ RECORD 4 ]
a | 3
b | 2
c | 1
-[ RECORD 5 ]
a | 2
b | 3
c | 1
-[ RECORD 6 ]
a | 2
b | 1
c | 3
```

This works well, but does seem a bit verbose for what is a pretty simple operation. This is due to the fact that we can't directly call RETURN NEXT a.b.c, but need to first assign values to variables declared by the INOUT incantations. We also want to avoid the even clumsier syntax of `tmp = a; a = b; b = tmp`.

Due to design decisions in the PL/pgSQL language, there is currently no good way to construct the return structure at runtime, that is, no RETURN a,b,c.

However, let's try to do it anyway and see what happens.

Using RETURNS TABLE

You might think that if there are no visible OUT parameters in a function declared as RETURNS TABLE(...), the following code might work:

```
CREATE FUNCTION permutations2(a int, b int, c int)
  RETURNS TABLE(a int, b int, c int)
AS $$
BEGIN
    RETURN NEXT a,b,c;
END;
$$ LANGUAGE plpgsql;
```

But when trying to do it this way, we get an error:

```
ERROR:  parameter name "a" used more than once
CONTEXT:  compilation of PL/pgSQL function "permutations2" near
  line 1
```

This error hints that the fields in the return table definition are also actually just OUT parameters and the whole RETURNS TABLE syntax is just another way to spell CREATE FUNCTION f(OUT ..., OUT...) RETURNS RECORD ....

This can be further verified by changing input parameters so that the definition can be fed into PostgreSQL:

```
CREATE FUNCTION permutations2(ia int, ib int, ic int)
  RETURNS TABLE(a int, b int, c int)
AS $$
BEGIN
    RETURN NEXT a,b,c;
END;
$$ LANGUAGE plpgsql;
```

And when we try to create this, we get the following output:

```
ERROR:  RETURN NEXT cannot have a parameter in function with OUT
  parameters
LINE 5:     RETURN NEXT a,b,c;
                        ^
```

So yes, the fields of the table in the RETURNS definition are actually just OUT parameters. We can try one last thing to get the function to construct the return structure in the RETURN NEXT clause.

```
CREATE TYPE abc AS (a int, b int, c int);

CREATE FUNCTION permutations2(ia int, ib int, ic int)
  RETURNS SETOF abc
AS $$
BEGIN
    RETURN NEXT a,b,c;
END;
$$ LANGUAGE plpgsql;
```

And running the previous code yields the following output:

```
ERROR:  RETURN NEXT must specify a record or row variable in
  function returning row
LINE 5:     RETURN NEXT a,b,c;
                        ^
```

Ok, this can't be done in this way either.

Fortunately, this is just a limitation of the PL/pgSQL language when creating the RETURN value and not a PostgreSQL limitation. In the next chapter we see that, for example, PL/Python can return complex data types in several ways without any problems.

Returning with no predefined structure

Sometimes, you really do need to write a function where the return structure is unknown. One nice thing about PostgreSQL function declarations is that you can use the return type RECORD, which can be left undefined up to the moment the function is called.

```
CREATE OR REPLACE FUNCTION run_a_query(query TEXT)
  RETURNS SETOF RECORD
AS $$
DECLARE
    retval RECORD;
BEGIN
    FOR retval IN EXECUTE query LOOP
        RETURN NEXT retval;
    END LOOP ;
END;
$$ LANGUAGE PLPGSQL;
```

This is a function that lets a user execute a query; quite useless as such, but it could be used as the basis for more useful functions that, for example, let users run queries only at a certain time, or performs some checks on queries before running them.

If you try to simply run the query:

```
select * from run_a_query('select usename, usesysid from
   pg_user');
```

You will get the following error:

```
ERROR:  a column definition list is required for functions
   returning "record"
LINE 1: select * from run_a_query('select usename, usesysid from
   pg_...
                                   ^
```

To use this kind of function, you need to tell PostgreSQL what the return values will be by adding a column definition list at call time in the following way:

```
select * from run_a_query('select usename,usesysid from pg_user')
   as ("user" text, uid int);
```

So will this work? No, you will get the following error:

```
ERROR:  wrong record type supplied in RETURN NEXT
DETAIL:  Returned type name does not match expected type text in
   column 1.
CONTEXT:  PL/pgSQL function run_a_query(text) line 6 at RETURN
   NEXT
```

Changing things a little more, we finally arrive at something that works.

```
hannu=# select * from run_a_query('select usename::text,usesysid::int
from pg_user') as
   ("user" text, uid int);
-[ RECORD 1 ]--
user | postgres
uid  | 10
-[ RECORD 2 ]--
user | hannu
uid  | 17573
```

What do we learn from this? PostgreSQL will let you return an arbitrary record from a function, but it is very particular in how it does it. When you call the function, you will need to be very deliberate about things, especially data types. PostgreSQL will use default casts to convert data to different data types if it knows enough information. But in a function such as this, much of that information is not known.

Returning SETOF ANY

There is another way to define functions which can operate on and return incomplete type definitions, the ANY* pseudo-types.

Let's define a function, which turns a simple one-dimensional PostgreSQL array of any type into a set of rows with one element of the same type.

```
CREATE OR REPLACE FUNCTION array_to_rows( array_in ANYARRAY )
  RETURNS TABLE(row_out ANYELEMENT)
AS $$
BEGIN
    FOR i IN 1.. array_upper(array_in,1) LOOP
        row_out =  array_in[i];
        RETURN NEXT ;
    END LOOP;
END;
$$ LANGUAGE plpgsql;
```

This work nicely on an array of integers.

```
hannu=# select array_to_rows('{1,2,3}'::int[]);
-[ RECORD 1 ]-+--
array_to_rows | 1
-[ RECORD 2 ]-+--
array_to_rows | 2
-[ RECORD 3 ]-+--
array_to_rows | 3
```

It also works nicely on an array of dates.

```
hannu=# select array_to_rows('{"1970-1-1","2012-12-12"}'::date[]);
-[ RECORD 1 ]-+-----------
array_to_rows | 1970-01-01
-[ RECORD 2 ]-+-----------
array_to_rows | 2012-12-12
```

It even works on arrays of records from user-defined tables.

```
hannu=# create table mydata(id serial primary key, data text);
NOTICE:  CREATE TABLE will create implicit sequence
  "mydata_id_seq" for serial column "mydata.id"
NOTICE:  CREATE TABLE / PRIMARY KEY will create implicit index
  "mydata_pkey" for table "mydata"
CREATE TABLE

hannu=# insert into mydata values(1, 'one'), (2,'two');
```

```
INSERT 0 2
hannu=# select array_to_rows(array(select m from mydata m));
-[ RECORD 1 ]-+--------
array_to_rows | (1,one)
-[ RECORD 2 ]-+--------
array_to_rows | (2,two)

hannu=# select * from array_to_rows
   (array(select m from mydata m));
-[ RECORD 1 ]
id   | 1
data | one
-[ RECORD 2 ]
id   | 2
data | two
```

The two last `select` statements return a one-column table of type `mydata`, and a two-column table of the same expanded into its component columns. This single function was flexible enough to handle several different types of data without any changes.

> There is a more potent version of `array_to_rows` built into PostgreSQL called `unnest()`. The built-in function is faster than our sample one and can also deal with arrays with more than one dimension:
>
> ```
> hannu=# select unnest('{{1,2,3}, {4,5,6}}'::int[]);
> -[ RECORD 1 ]
> unnest | 1
> -[ RECORD 2 ]
> unnest | 2
> -[ RECORD 3 ]
> unnest | 3
> -[ RECORD 4 ]
> unnest | 4
> -[ RECORD 5 ]
> unnest | 5
> -[ RECORD 6 ]
> unnest | 6
> ```

PostgreSQL has a weird array type, which can hold arrays of any number of dimensions. It is even weirder than that, as the array slices in any dimension can also start at any positive index (and they are by default 1-based). For example, an array with indices ranging from -2 to 2 is produced by the following incantation:

```
hannu=# select '[-2:2]={1,2,3,4,5}'::int[];
-[ RECORD 1 ]------------
int4 | [-2:2]={1,2,3,4,5}
```

To check that this really is so, use the following code snippet:

```
hannu=# select array_dims('[-2:2]={1,2,3,4,5}'::int[]);
-[ RECORD 1 ]------
array_dims | [-2:2]
```

The third element of that array is 3, and that is the middle one.

Variadic argument lists

PostgreSQL also has a facility to write a function with a variable number of arguments. This is accomplished by using VARIADIC.

```
CREATE OR REPLACE FUNCTION unnest_v(VARIADIC arr anyarray)
  RETURNS SETOF anyelement AS $$
BEGIN
    RETURN QUERY SELECT unnest(arr);
END;
$$ LANGUAGE plpgsql;
```

The previous code snippet is another simple example with little real world value, but it shows how to construct a function with variable arguments.

```
hannu=# select unnest_v(1,2,3,4);
-[ RECORD 1 ]
unnest_v | 1
-[ RECORD 2 ]
unnest_v | 2
-[ RECORD 3 ]
unnest_v | 3
-[ RECORD 4 ]
unnest_v | 4
```

Summary of RETURN SETOF variants

We learned that you can return table-like data sets from a function using one of the following:

RETURNS ...	RECORD structure	INSIDE function
`SETOF <type>`	From type definition	DECLARE row variable of ROW or RECORD type
		ASSIGN to row variable
		RETURN NEXT var;
`SETOF <table/ view>`	Same as table or view structure	
`SETOF RECORD`	Dynamic, using AS (name type, …) at call site	
`SETOF RECORD`	Using `OUT` and `INOUT` function arguments. Assign to `OUT` variables.	
	`RETURN NEXT ;`	
`TABLE (...)`	Declared in-line in parentheses after `TABLE` keyword, converted to `OUT` variables for use in function. Assigned to `OUT` variables from the `TABLE(...)` part of the declaration.	
	`RETURN NEXT ;`	

Returning cursors

Another method of getting a tabular data out of function is by using a CURSOR.

CURSOR, or a portal as it is sometimes referenced in PostgreSQL documentation, is an internal structure which contains a prepared query plan ready to return rows from the query. Sometimes the cursor needs to retrieve all the data for the query at once, but for many queries it does lazy fetching. For example, queries that need to scan all of the data in a table such as SELECT * FROM xtable, only read as much data as needed for each FETCH from the cursor.

In plain SQL, CURSOR is defined as follows:

```
DECLARE mycursor CURSOR  FOR <query >;
```

And later the rows are fetched using the following statement:

```
FETCH NEXT FROM  mycursor;
```

While you can use a cursor to handle the data from a set returning function the usual way, by simply declaring the cursor as `DECLARE mycursor CURSOR  FOR SELECT * FROM mysetfunc();`, it is many times more beneficial to have the function itself just return a cursor.

You would want to do this if you need different cursors based on argument values, or if you need to return dynamically structured data out of a function without defining the structure when calling the function.

The cursor in PL/pgSQL is represented by a variable of type `refcursor` and must be declared in one of the following three ways:

```
DECLARE
    curs1 refcursor;
    curs2 CURSOR FOR SELECT * FROM tenk1;
    curs3 CURSOR (key integer) IS SELECT * FROM tenk1 WHERE
      unique1 = key;
```

The first variant declares an unbound cursor which needs to be bound to a query at OPEN time. The two remaining variants declare a cursor bound to a query.

You can read a good technical overview on using cursors in PL/pgSQL functions from the official PostgreSQL documentation at http://www.postgresql.org/docs/current/static/plpgsql-cursors.html.

One thing to note about the documentation is that you don't really need to "return" the cursor, at least not now.

The documentation states:

"The following example shows one way to return multiple cursors from a single function:

CREATE FUNCTION myfunc(refcursor, refcursor) RETURNS SETOF refcursor AS $$

BEGIN

*OPEN $1 FOR SELECT * FROM table_1;*

RETURN NEXT $1;

OPEN $2 FOR SELECT * FROM table_2;

RETURN NEXT $2;

END;

$$ LANGUAGE plpgsql;

-- need to be in a transaction to use cursors.

BEGIN;

SELECT * FROM myfunc('a', 'b');

FETCH ALL FROM a;

FETCH ALL FROM b;

COMMIT;"

You could also write the function `myfunc` using `OUT` parameters:

```
CREATE FUNCTION myfunc2(cur1 refcursor, cur2 refcursor)
RETURNS VOID AS $$
BEGIN
    OPEN cur1 FOR SELECT * FROM table_1;
    OPEN cur2 FOR SELECT * FROM table_2;
END;
$$ LANGUAGE plpgsql;
```

You would still run the function exactly the same as the function returning the cursor variable.

Iterating over cursors returned from another function

To wrap up our cursors discussion, let's go through an example of returning a cursor and then iterating over the returned cursor in another PL/pgSQL function:

1. First, let's create a five row table and fill it with data:

    ```
    create table fiverows(id serial primary key, data text);
    insert into fiverows(data) values ('one'), ('two'),
                    ('three'), ('four'), ('five');
    ```

2. Next, let's define our cursor returning function. This function will open a cursor for a query based on its argument and then returns that cursor:

```
CREATE FUNCTION curtest1(cur refcursor, tag text)
  RETURNS refcursor
AS $$
BEGIN
    OPEN cur FOR SELECT id, data || '+' || tag FROM
       fiverows;
    RETURN cur;
END;
$$ LANGUAGE plpgsql;
```

3. Next, we define a function which uses the function we just created to open two additional cursors and then process the query results. To show we are not cheating and that the function really creates the cursors, we use the function twice and iterate over the results in parallel:

```
CREATE FUNCTION curtest2(tag1 text, tag2 text)
  RETURNS SETOF fiverows
AS $$
DECLARE
    cur1 refcursor;
    cur2 refcursor;
    row record;
BEGIN
    cur1 = curtest1(NULL, tag1);
    cur2 = curtest1(NULL, tag2);
    LOOP
        FETCH cur1 INTO row;
        EXIT WHEN NOT FOUND ;
        RETURN NEXT row;
        FETCH cur2 INTO row;
        EXIT WHEN NOT FOUND ;
        RETURN NEXT row;
    END LOOP;
END;
$$ LANGUAGE plpgsql;
```

By passing in NULL to the first parameters of curtest1, PostgreSQL automatically generates the cursor names so that multiple invocations of this function will not get name conflicts with any other functions which also create cursors.

Wrap up of functions returning a cursor(s)

The pros of using cursors are as follows:

- Cursors are a useful tool if you don't want to always execute the query and wait for the full resultset before returning from a function

- They are also the only way currently to return multiple resultsets out of a user-defined function

The cons of using cursors are as follows:

- They mainly work for passing data between functions on the server and you are still limited to one recordset per call returned to the database client

- They are sometimes confusing to use, and bound and unbound cursors are not always interchangeable

Other ways to work with structured data

We now have covered the traditional ways of returning sets of structured data from functions. We will now start with the more interesting part. Other methods of passing around complex data structures have evolved in the world today.

Complex data types for modern world – XML and JSON

In the real world, most of the data is not in a single table and the database is not the main thing that most programmers focus on. Often, they don't even think of it at all, or at least would rather not think about it.

If you are a database developer working on the database side of things, it is often desirable to talk to the clients (be it web or application developers as your client, or programs as database clients) in the language they speak. Currently, the two most widely spoken data languages by the web applications and their developers are XML and JSON.

Both XML and JSON are text-based data formats, and as such, they can be easily saved into fields of type text. PostgreSQL, being a DBMS built for being user-extendable, also has extensive support for both of these formats.

XML data type and returning data as XML from functions

One of the extensions added to PostgreSQL to support XML data is a native XML data type. While the XML data type is largely just a text field, it does differ from text in the following ways:

- The XML stored in an XML field is checked to be well formed
- There are support functions for producing and working with known well-formed XML

An XML value can be produced in a couple of ways including the SQL standard method.

```
XMLPARSE ( { DOCUMENT | CONTENT } value)
```

PostgreSQL also has a specific syntax that will also produce an XML value.

```
xml '<foo>bar</foo>'
'<foo>bar</foo>'::xml
```

An XML value can be easily converted to a text representation by using the XMLSERIALIZE function.

```
XMLSERIALIZE ( { DOCUMENT | CONTENT } value AS type )
```

Additionally, PostgreSQL allows you to simply cast the XML value as text.

 The full description of the XML data type and it's associated functions is at http://www.postgresql.org/docs/current/static/datatype-xml.html. As each version of PostgreSQL has improved, the support for XML has also improved.

There are several *_to_xml functions in PostgreSQL, which take as input either a SQL query or a table or view and return its corresponding XML representation.

Let's look at this using the fiverows table we defined previously in the cursors section.

First, let's get the table data as XML:

```
hannu=# select table_to_xml('fiverows',true, false, '') as s;
-[ RECORD 1 ]------------------------------------------------
s | <fiverows xmlns:xsi="http://www.w3.org/2001/XMLSchema-
  instance">
  |
```

```
| <row>
|    <id>1</id>
|    <data>one</data>
| </row>
|
| <row>
|    <id>2</id>
|    <data>two</data>
| </row>
|
| <row>
|    <id>3</id>
|    <data>three</data>
| </row>
|
| <row>
|    <id>4</id>
|    <data>four</data>
| </row>
|
| <row>
|    <id>5</id>
|    <data>five</data>
| </row>
|
| </fiverows>
|
```

If you have a client that can handle XML, then the `*_to_xml` functions can be the way to return your complex data.

Another nice thing about `*_to_xml` functions is that you can create a function which returns several different XML documents in one go, and thus return data rows with different structures. A good example would be a payment order and rows, where the first record returned by the function is the XML for the order header followed by one or more records of XML for order rows, all returned from the same function in one call.

There are currently five variants of `*_to_xml` functions:

```
cursor_to_xml(cursor refcursor, count integer,
              nulls bool, tableforest bool, targetns text)
query_to_xml(query text,
              nulls bool, tableforest bool, targetns text)
table_to_xml(tbl regclass,
              nulls boolean, tableforest boolean, targetns text)
schema_to_xml(schema name,
```

```
                    nulls boolean, tableforest boolean, targetns text)
    database_to_xml(nulls boolean, tableforest bool, targetns text)
```

The `cursor_to_xml(...)` function which iterates over an open cursor is recommended for large data sets, as it can convert the data in chunks of rows without first accumulating all data in memory.

The next three functions return a string representing either a SQL query, a table name, or a schema name, and return all data from the named object. The `table_to_xml()` function also works on views. Then there is the `database_to_xml(...)` function which converts all of the current database to XML document. However, a common result of running it on a production database is an out of memory error:

```
hannu=# select database_to_xml(true, true, 'n');
ERROR:  out of memory
DETAIL:  Failed on request of size 1024.
```

Returning data in the JSON format

In PostgreSQL 9.2, there is a new native data type for JSON values. This new support for JSON is following the same growth pattern as XML. It initially started with two functions for converting arrays and records to JSON format, but in PostgreSQL 9.3 there will be more functions.

The current functions are `row_to_json(record, bool)` for converting any record to JSON, and `array_to_json(anyarray, bool)` for converting any array to JSON.

The following are some simple examples of using these functions:

```
hannu=# select array_to_json(array[1,2,3]);
-[ RECORD 1 ]-+--------
array_to_json | [1,2,3]

hannu=# select * from test;
-[ RECORD 1 ]--------------------
id      | 1
data    | 0.26281
tstampt | 2012-04-05 13:21:03.235
-[ RECORD 2 ]--------------------
id      | 2
data    | 0.1574
tstampt | 2012-04-05 13:21:05.201

hannu=# select row_to_json(t) from test t;
```

```
-[ RECORD 1 ]----------------------------------------------
-------
row_to_json | {"id":1,"data":0.26281,"tstampt":"2012-04-05
   13:21:03.235"}
-[ RECORD 2 ]----------------------------------------------
-------
row_to_json | {"id":2,"data":0.1574,"tstampt":"2012-04-05
   13:21:05.201"}
```

These functions are very useful as they enable us to write functions returning data much more complex than would be possible using the standard RETURNS TABLE syntax, but the real power of these functions comes from being able to convert arbitrarily complex rows.

Let's first create a simple table with some data:

```
create table test(
    id serial primary key,
    data text,
    tstamp timestamp default current_timestamp
);
insert into test(data) values(random()), (random());
```

Now, let's create another table, which has one column with the data type of the previous table, and insert rows from that table in the new table:

```
hannu=# create table test2(
hannu(#     id serial primary key,
hannu(#     data2 test,
hannu(#     tstamp timestamp default current_timestamp
hannu(# );
hannu=# insert into test2(data2) select test from test;
INSERT 0 2

hannu=# select * from test2;
-[ RECORD 1 ]-----------------------------------
id     | 5
data2  | (1,0.26281,"2012-04-05 13:21:03.235204")
tstamp | 2012-04-30 15:42:11.757535
-[ RECORD 2 ]-----------------------------------
id     | 6
data2  | (2,0.15740,"2012-04-05 13:21:05.2033")
tstamp | 2012-04-30 15:42:11.757535
```

Now, let's see how `row_to_json()` handles that:

```
hannu=# select row_to_json(t2, true) from test2 t2;
                            row_to_json
-----------------------------------------------------------
 {"id":5,
  "data2":{"id":1,"data":"0.26281",
           "tstamp":"2012-04-05 13:21:03.235204"},
  "tstamp":"2012-04-30 15:42:11.757535"}
 {"id":6,
  "data2":{"id":2,"data":"0.15740",
           "tstamp":"2012-04-05 13:21:05.2033"},
  "tstamp":"2012-04-30 15:42:11.757535"}
(2 rows)
```

The result was converted to JSON with no problems.

Just to be sure, let's push the complexity up a bit more and create a table test3, which has an array of table2 rows as its data value:

```
create table test3(
    id serial primary key,
    data3 test2[],
    tstamp timestamp default current_timestamp
);
insert into test3(data3)
select array(select test2 from test2);
```

Let's see if `row_to_json` still works:

```
select row_to_json(t3, true) from test3 t3;
------------------------------------------
{"id":1,
 "data3":[ {"id":1,
            "data2":{"id":1,
                     "data":"0.262814193032682",
                     "tstamp":"2012-04-05 13:21:03.235204"},
            "tstamp":"2012-04-05 13:25:03.644497"
           },
           {"id":2,
            "data2":{"id":2,
                     "data":"0.157406373415142",
                     "tstamp":"2012-04-05 13:21:05.2033"},
            "tstamp":"2012-04-05 13:25:03.644497"
           }
         ],
 "tstamp":"2012-04-16 14:40:15.795947"}
(1 row)
```

Yes it does!

Well, actually I had to manually format it a little, as the `prettyprint` flag to `row_to_json()` only forks for top level, and the second row of the result (the one following `"data3"`) was all on one line. But JSON itself was completely functional!

Summary

The main points we learned in this chapter are:

- You can return multiple rows
- You can return multiple rows of complex data, similar to a SELECT query
- You can return several sets of tables and have them possibly evaluated in a lazy manner by using refcursors
- You can return data as complex as you want using either XML or JSON

So there really are very few reasons for not using database functions as your main interaction mechanism with the database. In the next chapter, we will learn how to call functions when different types of events occur in the database.

5
PL/pgSQL Trigger Functions

While it is generally a good practice to keep related code together and avoid "hidden" actions as part of main application code flows, there are also valid cases where it is a good practice to add some kind of general or cross-application functionality to the database using automated actions which happen each and every time a table is modified. That is, the actions are part of your data model and not your application code and you want to be sure that it is not possible to forget or bypass them in a similar way that constraints make it impossible to insert invalid data.

The tool for adding automated function calls to a table modifying event is called a trigger. Triggers are especially useful for cases where there are multiple different client applications — possibly from different sources and using different programming styles — accessing the same data using multiple different functions or straight SQL.

In PostgreSQL a trigger is defined in two steps:

1. Define a trigger function using CREATE FUNCTION
2. Bind this trigger function to a table using CREATE TRIGGER

Creating the trigger function

The trigger function definition looks mostly like an ordinary function definition, except that it has a return value type trigger, and it does not take any arguments:

```
CREATE FUNCTION mytriggerfunc() RETURNS trigger AS $$ …
```

Trigger functions are passed information about their calling environment through a special TriggerData structure, which in the case of PL/pgSQL is accessible through a set of local variables. The local variables, OLD and NEW, represent the row the trigger is in the before and after states of the triggering event. Additionally, there are several other local variables starting with the prefix TG_ such as TG_WHEN or TG_TABLE_NAME for general context. Once your trigger function is defined, you can bind it to a specific set of actions on a table.

Creating the trigger

The simplified syntax for creating a user-defined TRIGGER statement is given as follows:

```
CREATE TRIGGER name
    { BEFORE | AFTER | INSTEAD OF } { event [ OR ... ] }
    ON table_name
    [ FOR [ EACH ] { ROW | STATEMENT } ]
    EXECUTE PROCEDURE function_name ( arguments )
```

In the preceding code the event is one of INSERT, UPDATE, DELETE, or TRUNCATE. There are a few more options which we will come back to in a later section.

The "arguments" seemingly passed to the trigger function in the trigger definition are not used as arguments when calling the trigger. Instead, they are available to trigger function as a text array (text []) in variable TG_ARGV (length of this array is in TG_NARGS). Let's start slowly investigating how triggers and trigger functions work.

First, we will use a simple trigger example and move to more complex examples step-by-step.

Simple "Hey, I'm called" trigger

The first trigger we work on simply sends back a notice to the database client each time the trigger is fired and provides some feedback on its firing conditions:

```
CREATE OR REPLACE FUNCTION notify_trigger()
  RETURNS TRIGGER AS $$
BEGIN
    RAISE NOTICE 'Hi, I got % invoked FOR % % % on %',
                             TG_NAME,
                             TG_LEVEL,
                             TG_WHEN,
                             TG_OP,
                             TG_TABLE_NAME;
END;
$$ LANGUAGE plpgsql;
```

Next, we need a table to bind this function to the following:

```
CREATE TABLE notify_test(i int);
```

And we are ready to define the trigger. As we try to be simple here, we define a trigger which is invoked on INSERT and which calls the function once on each row:

```
CREATE TRIGGER notify_insert_trigger
  AFTER INSERT ON notify_test
  FOR EACH ROW
EXECUTE PROCEDURE notify_trigger();Let's test it out.postgres=# INSERT
INTO notify_test VALUES(1),(2);
NOTICE:  Hi, I got notify_insert_trigger invoked FOR ROW AFTER INSERT
on notify_test
ERROR:  control reached end of trigger procedure without RETURN
CONTEXT:  PL/pgSQL function notify_trigger()
```

Hmm. It seems we need to return something from the function even though it is not needed for our purposes. The function definition says CREATE FUNCTION ... RETURNS trigger but we definitely cannot return a trigger from a function.

Back to the documentation!

OK, here it is. The trigger needs to return a value of a ROW or RECORD type and it is ignored in AFTER triggers. For now, let's just return NEW as this is the right type and always present even though it will be NULL in the DELETE trigger:

```
CREATE OR REPLACE FUNCTION notify_trigger()
RETURNS TRIGGER AS $$
BEGIN
    RAISE NOTICE 'Hi, I got % invoked FOR % % % on %',
                                TG_NAME,
                                TG_LEVEL, TG_WHEN, TG_OP, TG_TABLE_
NAME;
    RETURN NEW;
END;
$$ LANGUAGE plpgsql;
```

We could have equally well used RETURN NULL; here as the return value of AFTER triggers is ignored anyway:

```
A new test:postgres=# INSERT INTO notify_test VALUES(1),(2);
NOTICE:  Hi, I got notify_insert_trigger invoked FOR ROW AFTER INSERT
on notify_test
NOTICE:  Hi, I got notify_insert_trigger invoked FOR ROW AFTER INSERT
on notify_test
INSERT 0 2
```

As we see, the trigger function is indeed called once for each row inserted, so let's use the same function to also report UPDATE and DELETE functions:

```
CREATE TRIGGER notify_update_trigger
  AFTER UPDATE ON notify_test
  FOR EACH ROW
EXECUTE PROCEDURE notify_trigger();

CREATE TRIGGER notify_delete_trigger
  AFTER DELETE ON notify_test
  FOR EACH ROW
EXECUTE PROCEDURE notify_trigger();
```

Check if the preceding code works.

First, let's test the update trigger:

```
postgres=# update notify_test set i = i * 10;
NOTICE:  Hi, I got notify_update_trigger invoked FOR ROW AFTER UPDATE
on notify_test
NOTICE:  Hi, I got notify_update_trigger invoked FOR ROW AFTER UPDATE
on notify_test
UPDATE 2
```

Works fine—we get a notice for two invocations of our trigger function.

And now delete:

```
postgres=# delete from notify_test;
NOTICE:  Hi, I got notify_delete_trigger invoked FOR ROW AFTER DELETE
on notify_test
NOTICE:  Hi, I got notify_delete_trigger invoked FOR ROW AFTER DELETE
on notify_test
DELETE 2
```

If we only want to be notified each time an operation is performed on the table, the preceding code is enough. One small improvement can be made in how we define the triggers. Instead, of creating one trigger for each of INSERT, UPDATE, or DELETE, we can create a single trigger to be called for any of them. So let's replace the previous three triggers with just the following:

```
CREATE TRIGGER notify_trigger
  AFTER INSERT OR UPDATE OR DELETE
  ON notify_test
  FOR EACH ROW
EXECUTE PROCEDURE notify_trigger();
```

The ability to put more than one of INSERT, OR UPDATE, OR DELETE in the same trigger definition is a PostgreSQL extension to SQL standard. Since the action part of the trigger definition is non-standard anyway, especially when using a PL/pgSQL trigger function, this should not be a problem.

Let's now drop the individual triggers truncate the table and test again:

```
postgres=# DROP TRIGGER notify_insert_trigger ON notify_test;
DROP TRIGGER
postgres=# DROP TRIGGER notify_update_trigger ON notify_test;
DROP TRIGGER
postgres=# DROP TRIGGER notify_delete_trigger ON notify_test;
DROP TRIGGER
postgres=# TRUNCATE notify_test;
TRUNCATE TABLE
postgres=# INSERT INTO notify_test VALUES(1);
NOTICE:  Hi, I got notify_trigger invoked FOR ROW AFTER INSERT on
notify_test
INSERT 0 1
```

Works fine, but this reveals one weakness: we did not get any notification on TRUNCATE!

Unfortunately, we cannot simply add OR TRUNCATE in the preceding trigger definition. The TRUNCATE command does not act on single rows, and so FOR EACH ROW triggers make no sense for truncate and are not supported.

You need to have a separate trigger definition for TRUNCATE. Fortunately, we can still use the same function, at least for this simple "Hey, I'm called!" trigger:

```
CREATE TRIGGER notify_truncate_trigger
  AFTER TRUNCATE ON notify_test
  FOR EACH STATEMENT
EXECUTE PROCEDURE notify_trigger();
```

And now we get a notification on TRUNCATE as well:

```
postgres=# TRUNCATE notify_test;
NOTICE:  Hi, I got notify_truncate_trigger invoked FOR STATEMENT AFTER
TRUNCATE on notify_test
TRUNCATE TABLE
```

While getting these messages at each **Data Management Language** (DML) operation is cool, it has little production value.

So, let's develop this a bit further and log the event in an audit log table instead of sending something back to the user.

The audit trigger

One of the most common uses of triggers is logging data changes to tables in a consistent and transparent manner. When creating an audit trigger, we first must decide what we want to log.

A logical set of things that can be logged are: who changed the data, when the data was changed, and what operation changed the data. This information can be saved in the following table:

```
CREATE TABLE audit_log (
    username text, -- who did the change
    event_time_utc timestamp, -- when the event was recorded
    table_name text, -- contains schema-qualified table name
    operation text, -- INSERT, UPDATE, DELETE or TRUNCATE
    before_value json, -- the OLD tuple value
    after_value json -- the NEW tuple value
);
```

Some additional explanations on what we will log are as follows:

- The username will get the SESSION_USER variable, so we know who was logged in and not which role he had potentially assumed using SET ROLE.

- event_time_utc will contain the event time converted to **Coordinated Universal Time(UTC)** so that all strange date arithmetic around daylight saving change times can be avoided.

- table_name will be in format schema.table.

- Operation will be directly from TG_OP, though it could be just the first character (I/U/D/T) without losing any information.

- Finally, the before and after images of rows are stored as rows converted to json which is available as its own data type starting PostgreSQL Version 9.2 for easy human-readable representation of ROW values.

Next, the trigger function:

```
CREATE OR REPLACE FUNCTION audit_trigger()
  RETURNS trigger AS $$
DECLARE
    old_row json := NULL;
    new_row json := NULL;
BEGIN
    IF TG_OP IN ('UPDATE','DELETE') THEN
        old_row = row_to_json(OLD);
```

```
      END IF;
      IF TG_OP IN ('INSERT','UPDATE') THEN
          new_row = row_to_json(NEW);
      END IF;
      INSERT INTO  audit_log(
          username,
          event_time_utc,
          table_name,
          operation,
          before_value,
          after_value
      ) VALUES (
          session_user,
          current_timestamp AT TIME ZONE 'UTC',
          TG_TABLE_SCHEMA ||  '.' || TG_TABLE_NAME,
          TG_OP,
          old_row,
          new_row
      );
      RETURN NEW;
  END;
  $$ LANGUAGE plpgsql;
```

> The conditional expressions of checking the operations at the beginning
> of the function is needed to overcome the fact that NEW and OLD are not
> NULL for DELETE and INSERT triggers correspondingly. Rather, they
> are unassigned. Using an unassigned variable in any other way except
> assigning to it in PL/pgSQL results in an error.

We are now ready to define our new logging trigger:

```
CREATE TRIGGER audit_log
  AFTER INSERT OR UPDATE OR DELETE
  ON notify_test
  FOR EACH ROW
EXECUTE PROCEDURE audit_trigger();
```

Running a small test, we remove our original notify triggers from the notify_test
table and perform a few simple operations:

```
postgres=# DROP TRIGGER notify_trigger ON notify_test;
DROP TRIGGER
postgres=# DROP TRIGGER notify_truncate_trigger ON notify_test;
DROP TRIGGER
postgres=# TRUNCATE notify_test;
```

```
TRUNCATE TABLE
postgres=# INSERT INTO notify_test VALUES (1);
INSERT 0 1
postgres=# UPDATE notify_test SET i = 2;
UPDATE 1
postgres=# DELETE FROM notify_test;
DELETE 1
postgres=# SELECT * FROM audit_log;
-[ RECORD 1 ]--+--------------------------
username       | postgres
event_time_utc | 2013-04-14 13:14:18.501529
table_name     | public.notify_test
operation      | INSERT
before_value   |
after_value    | {"i":1}
-[ RECORD 2 ]--+--------------------------
username       | postgres
event_time_utc | 2013-04-14 13:14:18.51216
table_name     | public.notify_test
operation      | UPDATE
before_value   | {"i":1}
after_value    | {"i":2}
-[ RECORD 3 ]--+--------------------------
username       | postgres
event_time_utc | 2013-04-14 13:14:18.52331
table_name     | public.notify_test
operation      | DELETE
before_value   | {"i":2}
after_value    |
```

This works well enough. Depending on your needs, this function will likely need some tweaking. Enough of just watching and recording of DML, it's time to start influencing what goes on there.

Disallowing DELETE

What if our business requirements are such that data can only be added and modified in some tables, but not deleted?

One way to handle this would be to just revoke the DELETE right on these tables from all users (remember to also revoke DELETE from PUBLIC), but this can also be achieved using triggers.

A generic cancel trigger can be written as follows:

```
CREATE OR REPLACE FUNCTION cancel_op()
  RETURNS TRIGGER AS $$
BEGIN
    IF TG_WHEN = 'AFTER' THEN
        RAISE EXCEPTION 'YOU ARE NOT ALLOWED TO % ROWS IN %.%',
                        TG_OP, TG_TABLE_SCHEMA, TG_TABLE_NAME;
    END IF;
    RAISE NOTICE '% ON ROWS IN %.% WON''T HAPPEN',
                        TG_OP, TG_TABLE_SCHEMA, TG_TABLE_NAME;
    RETURN NULL;
END;
$$ LANGUAGE plpgsql;
```

The same trigger function can be used for both BEFORE and AFTER triggers. If you use it as a BEFORE trigger the operation is skipped with a message, but if used as an AFTER trigger, an ERROR is raised and the current (sub) transaction is rolled back.

It would also be easy to add logging of the delete attempts into a table in this same trigger function to help enforce company policy — just add INSERT to a log table similar to the previous example.

Of course, you can make one or both messages more menacing if you want, by adding something as "Authorities will be notified!" or "You will be terminated!".

Let's take a look at how this works in the following code:

```
postgres=# CREATE TABLE delete_test1(i int);
CREATE TABLE
postgres=# INSERT INTO delete_test1 VALUES(1);
INSERT 0 1
postgres=# CREATE TRIGGER disallow_delete AFTER DELETE ON delete_test1
FOR EACH ROW  EXECUTE PROCEDURE cancel_op();
CREATE TRIGGER
postgres=# DELETE FROM delete_test1 WHERE i = 1;
ERROR:  YOU ARE NOT ALLOWED TO DELETE ROWS IN public.delete_
test1Notice that the AFTER trigger raised an error.postgres=# CREATE
TRIGGER skip_delete BEFORE DELETE ON delete_test1 FOR EACH ROW
EXECUTE PROCEDURE cancel_op();
CREATE TRIGGER
postgres=# DELETE FROM delete_test1 WHERE i = 1;
NOTICE:  DELETE ON ROWS IN public.delete_test1 WON'T HAPPEN
DELETE 0
```

This time, the BEFORE trigger canceled the delete and the AFTER trigger, though still there, was not reached.

The same trigger could also be used to enforce a no-update policy, or even disallow inserts to some table that has to have immutable contents.

Disallowing TRUNCATE

You may have noticed that the preceding trigger can easily be bypassed for DELETE if you delete everything using TRUNCATE.

While you cannot simply skip TRUNCATE by returning NULL (this works only for row-level BEFORE triggers), you still can make it impossible by raising an error if TRUNCATE is attempted. Create an AFTER trigger using the same function used previously for DELETE:

```
CREATE TRIGGER disallow_truncate
  AFTER TRUNCATE ON delete_test1
  FOR EACH STATEMENT
EXECUTE PROCEDURE cancel_op();
```

And here you are, with no more TRUNCATE:

```
postgres=# TRUNCATE delete_test1;
ERROR:  YOU ARE NOT ALLOWED TO TRUNCATE ROWS IN public.delete_test1
```

Of course, you could also raise the error in a BEFORE trigger, but then you would need to write your own unconditional raise-error trigger function instead of cancel_op().

Modifying the NEW record

Another form of auditing frequently used is to log information in fields in the same row as the data. As an example, let's define a trigger which logs the time and active user in fields last_changed_at and last_changed_by fields at each INSERT and UPDATE. In row-level BEFORE triggers you can modify what actually gets written by changing the NEW record. You can either assign values to some fields or even return a different record with the same structure. For example, if you return OLD from the UPDATE trigger, you effectively make sure that the row can't be updated.

Timestamping trigger

To form the basis of our audit logging in the table, we start with creating a trigger that sets the user who made the last change and when the change occurred:

```
CREATE OR REPLACE FUNCTION changestamp()
  RETURNS TRIGGER AS $$
BEGIN
    NEW.last_changed_by = SESSION_USER;
    NEW.last_changed_at = CURRENT_TIMESTAMP;
    RETURN NEW;
END;
$$ LANGUAGE plpgsql;
```

Of course, this works only on a table which has correct fields:

```
CREATE TABLE modify_test(
    id serial PRIMARY KEY,
    data text,
    created_by text default SESSION_USER,
    created_at timestamp default CURRENT_TIMESTAMP,
    last_changed_by text default SESSION_USER,
    last_changed_at timestamp default CURRENT_TIMESTAMP
);


CREATE TRIGGER changestamp
  BEFORE UPDATE ON modify_test
  FOR EACH ROW
EXECUTE PROCEDURE changestamp();
```

Now, let's take a look at our newly created trigger:

```
postgres=# INSERT INTO modify_test(data) VALUES('something');
INSERT 0 1
postgres=# UPDATE modify_test SET data = 'something else' WHERE id =
1;
UPDATE 1
postgres=# SELECT * FROM modify_test; -[ RECORD 1 ]---+--------------
-------------
id              | 1
data            | something else
created_by      | postgres
created_at      | 2013-04-15 09:28:23.966179
last_changed_by | postgres
last_changed_at | 2013-04-15 09:28:31.937196
```

Immutable fields trigger

When you are depending on the fields in the rows as part of your audit record, you need to ensure that the values reflect reality. We were able to make sure that the last_changed_ * fields always contain the correct value, but how about the created_by and created_at values? These can easily be changed in later updates, but they should never change. Even initially, they can be set to false values, since default values can be easily overridden by giving any other value in the INSERT statement.

So, let's modify our changestamp() trigger function into a usagestamp() function, which makes sure that initial values are what they should be and that they stay like that:

```
CREATE OR REPLACE FUNCTION usagestamp()
  RETURNS TRIGGER AS $$
BEGIN
    IF TG_OP = 'INSERT' THEN
        NEW.created_by = SESSION_USER;
        NEW.created_at = CURRENT_TIMESTAMP;
    ELSE
        NEW.created_by = OLD.created_by;
        NEW.created_at = OLD.created_at;
    END IF;

    NEW.last_changed_by = SESSION_USER;
    NEW.last_changed_at = CURRENT_TIMESTAMP;
    RETURN NEW;
END;
$$ LANGUAGE plpgsql;
```

In case of INSERT, we set created_* fields to the needed values regardless of what the INSERT query tries to set them to. In case of UPDATE, we just carry over the old values, again overriding any attempted changes.

This function then needs to be used for creating a BEFORE INSERT OR UPDATE trigger:

```
CREATE TRIGGER usagestamp
  BEFORE INSERT OR UPDATE ON modify_test
  FOR EACH ROW
EXECUTE PROCEDURE usagestamp();
```

Now, let's test out trying to update the created audit log information. First, we will need to drop the original trigger so we don't have two trigger firing on the same table. Then, we will try to change the values of `created_by` and `created_at`:

```
postgres=# DROP TRIGGER changestamp ON modify_test;
DROP TRIGGER
postgres=# UPDATE modify_test SET created_by = 'notpostgres',
created_at = '2000-01-01';
UPDATE 1
postgres=# select * from modify_test;
-[ RECORD 1 ]---+---------------------------
id              | 1
data            | something else
created_by      | postgres
created_at      | 2013-04-15 09:28:23.966179
last_changed_by | postgres
last_changed at | 2013-04-15 09:33:25.386006
```

Looking at the results, you can see that the created information is still the same, but the last changed information has been updated.

Controlling when a trigger is called

While it is relatively easy to perform trigger actions conditionally inside the PL/pgSQL trigger function, it is often more efficient to skip invoking the trigger altogether. The performance effects of firing a trigger is not generally noticed when only a few events are fired. However, if you are bulk loading data or updating large portions of your table, the cumulative effects can certainly be felt. To avoid the overhead, its best to only call the trigger function when it is actually needed.

There are two ways to narrow down when a trigger is called in the CREATE TRIGGER command itself.

So once more use the same syntax, but this time with all options:

```
CREATE TRIGGER name
    { BEFORE | AFTER | INSTEAD OF } { event [ OR event ... ] }
    [ OF column_name  [ OR column_name ... ] ] ON table_name
    [ FOR [ EACH ] { ROW | STATEMENT } ]
    [ WHEN ( condition ) ]
    EXECUTE PROCEDURE function_name ( arguments )
```

Conditional trigger

A flexible way of controlling triggers is a generic WHEN clause that is similar to WHERE in SQL queries. With a WHEN clause, you can write any expression, except a subquery, that is tested before the trigger function is called. The expression must result in a Boolean value, and if the value is FALSE (or NULL which is automatically converted to FALSE), the trigger function is not called.

For example, you could use this to enforce a "No updates on Friday afternoon" policy.

```
CREATE OR REPLACE FUNCTION cancel_with_message()
  RETURNS TRIGGER AS $$
BEGIN
    RAISE EXCEPTION '%', TG_ARGV[0];
    RETURN NULL;
END;
$$ LANGUAGE plpgsql;
```

This function just raises an exception with the string passed as an argument in the CREATE TRIGGER statement. Notice that we cannot use TG_ARGV[0] directly, as the message as the PL/pgSQL syntax requires a string constant as the third element of RAISE.

Using the previous trigger function, we can set up triggers to enforce various constraints by specifying both the condition (in the WHEN(...) clause) and the message to raise if this condition is met as the argument to trigger function:

```
CREATE TRIGGER no_updates_on_friday_afternoon
  BEFORE INSERT OR UPDATE OR DELETE OR TRUNCATE ON new_tasks
  FOR EACH STATEMENT
  WHEN (CURRENT_TIME > '12:00' AND extract(DOW from CURRENT_TIMESTAMP)
= 5)
EXECUTE PROCEDURE cancel_with_message('Sorry, we have a "No task
change on Friday afternoon" policy!');
```

Now if anybody tries to modify the new_tasks table on any Friday afternoon he gets a message about this policy:

```
postgres=# insert into new_tasks values (...);
ERROR:  Sorry, we have a "No task change on Friday afternoon" policy!
```

One thing to note about trigger arguments is that the argument list is always an array of text (text []).

All of the arguments given in the CREATE TRIGGER statement are converted to strings, and this includes any NULL values.

This means putting NULL in the argument list results in text NULL in the corresponding slot in PG_ARGV.

Trigger on specific field changes

Another way of controlling when a trigger is fired is using a list of columns. In UPDATE triggers, you can specify one or more comma-separated columns to tell PostgreSQL that the trigger function should only be executed if any of the listed columns change.

It is possible to construct the same conditional expression with a WHEN clause, but the list of columns has cleaner syntax:

```
WHEN (
    NEW.column1 IS DISTINCT FROM OLD.column1
    OR
    NEW.column2 IS DISTINCT FROM OLD.column2)
```

A common example of how this conditional expression is used is raising an error each time someone tries to change a primary key column. This can easily be done by declaring an AFTER trigger using the cancel_op() trigger function (defined previously in this chapter) as follows:

```
CREATE TRIGGER disallow_pk_change
  AFTER UPDATE OF id ON table_with_pk_id
  FOR EACH ROW
EXECUTE PROCEDURE cancel_op();
```

Visibility

Sometimes your trigger functions may run into the **Multiversion Concurrency Control (MVCC)** visibility rules of how PostgreSQL's system interacts with changes to data.

A function declared STABLE or IMMUTABLE will never see changes applied to the underlying table by previous triggers.

A VOLATILE function follows more complex rules, which are in a nutshell as follows:

- The statement-level BEFORE triggers see no changes made by the current statement, and statement-level AFTER triggers see all of the changes made by the statement.

- Data changes by the operation to the row causing the trigger to fire are of course not visible to BEFORE triggers, as the operation has not happened yet. Changes made by other triggers to other rows in the same statement are visible and as the order of the rows processed is undefined this needs caution!

- The same is true of INSTEAD OF triggers. The changes by the triggers fired in the same command on previous rows are visible to current invocation of trigger function. Row-level AFTER triggers are fired when all of the changes to all rows of the outer command are complete and visible to the trigger function.

This all applies to functions querying data in the database, the OLD and NEW rows are of course visible as described previously.

The same information in perhaps a different wording is available at
http://www.postgresql.org/docs/current/static/spi-visibility.html.

And most importantly – use triggers cautiously!

Triggers are an appropriate tool for using in database-side actions, such as auditing, logging, enforcing complex constraints, and even replication (there are several logical replication systems based of triggers in production use). However, for most application logic it is much better to avoid triggers as they can lead to really weird and hard to debug problems.

Variables passed to the PL/pgSQL TRIGGER function

The following is a complete list of variables available to a trigger function written in PL/pgSQL:

OLD, NEW	RECORD	before and after images of the row the trigger is called on. OLD is unassigned for INSERT and NEW is unassigned for DELETE.
		Both are UNASSIGNED in statement-level triggers.

TG_NAME	name	The name of the trigger (this and following from the trigger definition).
TG_WHEN	text	One of BEFORE, AFTER, or INSTEAD OF.
TG_LEVEL	text	ROW or STATEMENT.
TG_OP	text	One of INSERT, UPDATE, DELETE, or TRUNCATE.
TG_RELID	oid	OID of the table the trigger is created on.
TG_TABLE_NAME	name	The name of the table (old spelling TG_RELNAME is deprecated but still available).
TG_TABLE_SCHEMA	name	The schema name of the table.
TG_NARGS, TG_ARGV[]	Int, text[]	Number of arguments and the array of the arguments from trigger definition.

Summary

A trigger is a binding of a set of actions to certain operations performed on a table or view. This set of actions is defined in a special trigger function distinguished by specifying the type of returned value to be of special pseudotype trigger. So each time an operation (INSERT, UPDATE, DELETE, or TRUNCATE) is performed on the table, this trigger function is called by the system.

It can be executed either FOR EACH ROW or FOR EACH STATEMENT. If executed for each row (row level trigger), the function is passed special variables OLD and NEW. This will contain the row content, as it is currently in the database (OLD), and as it is at the moment the trigger function is called (NEW). Where the OLD or NEW value is missing, it is passed as undefined. If executed once per statement (the statement-level trigger), both OLD and NEW are unassigned for all operations.

The trigger function for row-level triggers on INSERT, UPDATE, and DELETE can be set to execute either BEFORE or AFTER the operation on a table and the INSTEAD OF operation on view.

The trigger function for statement level triggers on INSERT, UPDATE, and DELETE can be set to execute either BEFORE or AFTER the operation on both tables and views.

While TRUNCATE is logically a special form of "delete all" statement, no ON DELETE triggers will fire in case of TRUNCATE. Instead, you can use a special ON TRUNCATE trigger on the same table. Only statement-level on truncate triggers are possible. While you can't skip statement triggers by returning a NULL, you can RAISE EXCEPTION and abort the transaction.

It is also not possible to define any ON TRUNCATE triggers on views.

6
Debugging PL/pgSQL

This chapter is entirely optional. Since you have only produced the highest quality, bug-free code using the best possible algorithms, this text is probably a waste of your time. Of course your functions parse perfectly on the first try. Your views show exactly what they should—according to the enviously complete business and technical documentation that you wrote last month. There is no need for version control on your procedures, as there has only ever been a Version 1.

Since you are still reading this, I'm sure that you're a whole lot more like me. I spend about 10 percent of my time writing new code, and about 90 percent of it editing the mistakes and oversights that I (and others) made in the first 10 percent. In fact, it could be argued that no new code is ever written at all. Actually, a more accurate description of the process is that a dumb assertion is made, and then edited until the customer can no longer stand the **Quality Assurance (QA)** process. We then ship the result in the hopes of being useful to the end user. Was that too much reality for you? Sorry.

The objective of this chapter is to make you much faster at making mistakes. As a by-product, you will also learn how to diagnose and fix them at an alarming rate of speed. The net effect for which we are hoping is that your boss will assume you wrote it correctly the first time. This is, of course, a lie, but a very useful one.

This concept is critical to agile software development. In that philosophy, it is called "prototyping". The idea is to create a feature quickly and demonstrate it as a conversation point, rather than trying to produce an entire system (presumably perfectly) from conceptual documentation. Other authors refer to it as "failing quickly". It is a recognition that the first 3 or 4 development iterations will probably not be acceptable to the customer, and shouldn't be advertised as final until some discussion has occurred.

This process effectively requires the developer to "live" in the debugger. He continually changes the outputs and routines until the desired effect is achieved. PostgreSQL has a wonderful set of debugging tools available to help you fix your mess. Let me show you how they work.

"Manual" debugging with RAISE NOTICE

You might want to have a look at *Chapter 10, Publishing Your Code as PostgreSQL*. That chapter includes some samples (and an extremely handy way to install them) that will be useful here in this part of the book. The examples will be shown again here in the text of this chapter, but they would be quite a bit easier for you to install as an extension.

Here is the first promised example:

```
CREATE OR REPLACE FUNCTION format_us_full_name_debug(
                                    prefix text,
                                    firstname text,
                                    mi text,
                                    lastname text,
                                    suffix text)
  RETURNS text AS
$BODY$
DECLARE
  fname_mi text;
  fmi_lname text;
  prefix_fmil text;
  pfmil_suffix text;
BEGIN
  fname_mi := CONCAT_WS(' ', CASE trim(firstname) WHEN '' THEN NULL
ELSE firstname END, CASE trim(mi) WHEN '' THEN NULL ELSE mi END ||
'.');
  RAISE NOTICE 'firstname mi.: %', fname_mi;
  fmi_lname := CONCAT_WS(' ', CASE fname_mi WHEN '' THEN NULL ELSE
fname_mi END, CASE trim(lastname) WHEN '' THEN NULL ELSE lastname END);
  RAISE NOTICE 'firstname mi. lastname: %', fmi_lname;
  prefix_fmil := CONCAT_WS('. ', CASE trim(prefix) WHEN '' THEN NULL
ELSE prefix END, CASE fmi_lname WHEN '' THEN NULL ELSE fmi_lname END);
  RAISE NOTICE 'prefix. firstname mi lastname: %', prefix_fmil;
  pfmil_suffix := CONCAT_WS(', ', CASE prefix_fmil WHEN '' THEN NULL
ELSE prefix_fmil END, CASE trim(suffix) WHEN '' THEN NULL ELSE suffix
|| '.' END);
  RAISE NOTICE 'prefix. firstname mi lastname, suffix.: %', pfmil_
suffix;

  RETURN pfmil_suffix;
END;
$BODY$
  LANGUAGE plpgsql VOLATILE;
```

In this example, we format a person's full name using the magic of NULL propagation.

NULL propagation is what happens when any or all members of an expression are null. In the expression: `myvar := null || 'something'`, `myvar` will evaluate to `null`. PostgreSQL 9.1 introduces a very handy new function named `CONCAT_WS` (concatenate with separator) to take advantage of this effect.

For example:

```
lastfirst := CONCAT_WS(', ', lastname, firstname);
```

The preceding code will not print the comma and whitespace between `lastname` and `firstname` if either `firstname` or `lastname` is not present. This effect is used in the function `format_us_address()` with many levels of nesting to provide an address that is visually appealing as well as postal processing friendly.

There are several statements in the code example showing how to use `RAISE NOTICE` along with some text and a variable to provide debugging information as the function is being called. For example, running our function in `pgAdmin3` will produce some notification messages:

```
SELECT format_us_full_name_debug('Mr','Kirk','L','Roybal','Author');
```

You can see those messages in `pgAdmin3` in the **Messages** tab in the following screenshot:

```
Data Output   Explain   Messages   History
NOTICE:  firstname mi.: Kirk L.
NOTICE:  firstname mi. lastname: Kirk L. Roybal
NOTICE:  prefix. firstname mi lastname: Mr. Kirk L. Roybal
NOTICE:  prefix. firstname mi lastname, suffix.: Mr. Kirk L. Roybal, Author.


Total query runtime: 17 ms.
1 row retrieved.
```

The output of the same query in the command-line `psql` client is shown in the following code:

```
kroybal=# SELECT format_us_full_name_debug('Mr','Kirk','L','Roybal','Author');
NOTICE:  firstname mi.: Kirk L.
NOTICE:  firstname mi. lastname: Kirk L. Roybal
```

```
NOTICE:  prefix. firstname mi lastname: Mr. Kirk L. Roybal
NOTICE:  prefix. firstname mi lastname, suffix.: Mr. Kirk L. Roybal,
Author.
  format_us_full_name_debug
----------------------------
 Mr. Kirk L. Roybal, Author.
(1 row)
```

Throwing exceptions

The RAISE command takes several other operators than NOTICE. It will also throw exceptions that are intended for the calling code to catch. The following is an example of creating an exception:

```
CREATE OR REPLACE FUNCTION validate_us_zip(zipcode TEXT)
  RETURNS boolean
AS $$
DECLARE
  digits text;
BEGIN
  -- remove anything that is not a digit (POSIX compliantly, please)
  digits := (SELECT regexp_replace(zipcode,'[^[:digit:]]','','g'));

  IF digits = '' THEN
    RAISE EXCEPTION 'Zipcode does not contain any digits --> %',
digits USING HINT = 'Is this a US zip code?', ERRCODE = 'P9999';
  ELSIF length(digits) < 5 THEN
    RAISE EXCEPTION 'Zipcode does not contain enough digits --> %',
digits USING HINT = 'Zip code has less than 5 digits.', ERRCODE =
'P9998';
  ELSIF length(digits) > 9 THEN
    RAISE EXCEPTION 'Unnecessary digits in zip code --> %', digits
USING HINT = 'Zip code is more than 9 digits.', ERRCODE = 'P9997';
  ELSIF length(digits) > 5 AND length(digits) < 9 THEN
    RAISE EXCEPTION 'Zip code cannot be processed --> %', digits USING
HINT = 'Zip code abnormal length.', ERRCODE = 'P9996';
  ELSE
    RETURN true;
  END IF;
END;
$$ LANGUAGE plpgsql;
```

The ERRCODE values are defined by the developer. In this example, I used the general PL/pgSQL error code value (P0001 or plpgsql_error), started at the top of the range (P9999) of errors, and decremented for each type of error that I wished to expose. This is a very simplistic technique designed to prevent overlap in the future from error codes used by PL/pgSQL. You are free to invent any error codes you like, but would be well advised to avoid those already listed in the documentation at http://www.postgresql.org/docs/current/static/errcodes-appendix.html.

A sample function (error_trap_report) has been provided in the accompanying code that you can easily modify to determine the error code constant that is being thrown by any given error number. For PL/pgSQL functions, the error constant is plpgsql_error (P0001) by default.

The following is the code used to capture any errors thrown in the previous example:

```
CREATE OR REPLACE FUNCTION get_us_zip_validation_status(zipcode text)
returns text
AU
$$
BEGIN
  SELECT validate_us_zip(zipcode);
  RETURN 'Passed Validation';
EXCEPTION
  WHEN SQLSTATE 'P9999' THEN RETURN 'Non-US Zip Code';
  WHEN SQLSTATE 'P9998' THEN RETURN 'Not enough digits.';
  WHEN SQLSTATE 'P9997' THEN RETURN 'Too many digits.';
  WHEN SQLSTATE 'P9996' THEN RETURN 'Between 6 and 8 digits.';
  RAISE;  -- Some other SQL error.
END;
$$
LANGUAGE 'plpgsql';
```

This code can be called as follows:

```
SELECT get_us_zip_validation_status('34955');
 get_us_zip_validation_status
------------------------------
 Passed Validation
(1 row)

root=# SELECT get_us_zip_validation_status('349587');
 get_us_zip_validation_status
------------------------------
 Between 6 and 8 digits.
```

```
(1 row)

root=# SELECT get_us_zip_validation_status('3495878977');
 get_us_zip_validation_status
------------------------------
 Too many digits.
(1 row)

root=# SELECT get_us_zip_validation_status('BNHCGR');
 get_us_zip_validation_status
------------------------------
 Non-US Zip Code
(1 row)

root=# SELECT get_us_zip_validation_status('3467');
 get_us_zip_validation_status
------------------------------
 Not enough digits.
(1 row)
```

Logging to a file

The `RAISE` statement expression can be sent to a logfile using `log_min_messages`. This parameter is set in `postgresql.conf`. The valid values are: `debug5`, `debug4`, `debug3`, `debug2`, `debug1`, `info`, `notice`, `warning`, `error`, `log`, `fatal`, and `panic`.

The default logging level is packaging system dependent. On Ubuntu, the default logging level is `info`. The logging levels correspond to the same expressions for the `RAISE` statement. As a developer, you can raise any of the messages that are available and have them recorded in the file log for later analysis.

The simplest way to post a message to the PostgreSQL daemon logfile is with `RAISE LOG`:

```
RAISE LOG 'Why am I doing this?';
```

This logfile is usually located with the rest of the system logfiles under `/var/log`. On Ubuntu, this is `/var/log/postgresql/postgresql-9.1-main.log`.

Advantages of RAISE NOTICE

Using the RAISE NOTICE form of debugging has several advantages. It can be used easily and repeatedly with scripts for regression testing. This is very easily accomplished with the command-line client. Consider the following statement:

```
psql -qtc "SELECT format_us_full_name_debug('Mr','Kirk','L.','Roybal'
,'Author');"
```

The preceding statement produces the following output to stdout:

```
NOTICE:   firstname mi.: Kirk L..
NOTICE:   firstname mi. lastname: Kirk L.. Roybal
NOTICE:   prefix. firstname mi lastname: Mr. Kirk L.. Roybal
NOTICE:   prefix. firstname mi lastname, suffix.: Mr. Kirk L.. Roybal,
Author.
 Mr. Kirk L.. Roybal, Author.
```

Because a constant set of input parameters should always produce a known output, it is very easy to use command-line tools to test for expected outputs. When you are ready to deploy your newly modified code to the production system, run your command-line tests to verify that all of your functions still work as expected.

RAISE NOTICE is included with the product and requires no installation. This advantage will become clearer later in the chapter where the rather painful installation procedure for PL/pgSQL Debugger is explained.

The RAISE statement is easy to understand. The syntax is very straightforward and it is well documented at http://www.postgresql.org/docs/current/static/plpgsql-errors-and-messages.html.

RAISE works in any development environment and has been around for a very long time in almost every version of PostgreSQL on every operating system. I have used it with pgAdmin3, phpPgAdmin, as well as the command-line tool psql.

These attributes, taken together, make RAISE a very attractive tool for small-scale debugging.

Disadvantages of RAISE NOTICE

Unfortunately, there are some disadvantages to using this method of debugging. The primary disadvantage is remembering to remove the RAISE statements when they are no longer necessary. The messages tend to clutter up the psql command-line client, and are generally annoying to other developers. The log may fill up quickly with useless messages from previous debug sessions. RAISE statements need to be written, commented out, and restored when needed. They may not cover the actual bug being sought. They also slow down the execution of the routine.

Visual debugging

The PL/pgSQL Debugger is a project hosted on pgFoundry that provides a debugging interface into PostgreSQL Version 8.2 or higher. The following statement is mentioned at http://pgfoundry.org/projects/edb-debugger/:

> *"The PL/pgSQL debugger lets you step through PL/pgSQL code, set and clear breakpoints, view and modify variables, and walk through the call stack. "*

As you can see from the description, the PL/pgSQL Debugger can be quite a handy little tool to have in your arsenal.

Getting the debugger installed

Ok, now we move past the glamour, and need to actually get it running on your system. If you installed PostgreSQL with one of packages that contain the Debugger, installation is pretty simple. Otherwise, you will need to build it from source.

Building the PL/pgSQL Debugger from source is beyond the scope of this book. The best way to build the source would be to pull the latest version for the **Concurrent Versions System (CVS)** source control system and follow the README file in the directory. If you want to get started quickly with it, and you have a Windows machine available, the simplest way to use the Debugger is by using the Windows installer.

Installing pgAdmin3

The PL/pgSQL Debugger module works with pgAdmin3. There are no special steps necessary with the installation of pgAdmin3 for the debugger to function. Install it as usual from your package manager on the platform that you are using. For Ubuntu 10.04 LTS, the following is aptitude:

```
sudo apt-get install pgadmin3
```

Using the debugger

When the debugger is available for a particular database, it can be seen on the context menu when right-clicking on a PL/pgSQL function. We have already created some of those from the earlier part of this chapter. Using `format_us_full_name` as an example, right-click with the mouse and navigate to **Debugging | Debug**:

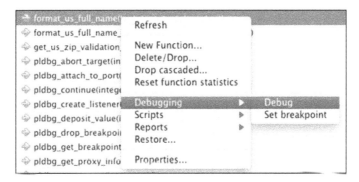

You will see the following dialog:

Enter some values into the columns, as seen in the preceding screenshot, and click on the **OK** button. You will be deposited into the debugger:

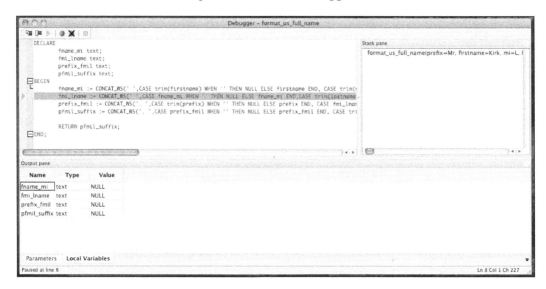

This will allow you to step through the code and see the values of any variables as they are being changed. Click on the "step-into" button a few times to watch how the values are modified as the function is performed:

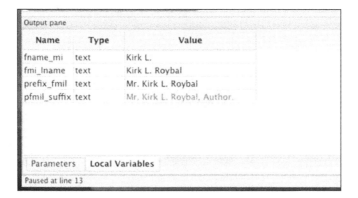

Advantages of the debugger

The PL/pgSQL Debugger does not require any resources on the server when not actually in use. Because it is invoked manually from within pgAdmin3, it is not resident in memory until it is actually called upon. This architecture does not require any background processes or additional daemons for the sake of debugging.

Also, the PL/pgSQL Debugger does not require any special "calling" function to be written to invoke the debugging process. There are no errors to trap, and no tables of error codes to interpret. Everything necessary to the debugging process is available in a simple window.

If you connect to your database as a `superuser`, you also have the ability to set a global break point. This break point can be set on any function or trigger and it will stop the next time any code path calls the function. This is particularly useful if you want to debug your functions or triggers in the context of your entire running application.

The greatest advantage of PL/pgSQL Debugger is that it does not require any special rigging in the functions that are being debugged. There is no code to insert or remove, and good coding practices do not need to be modified with respect to debugging. There is no possibility to "forget" the debugging code when moving to production. All of your PL/pgSQL functions are now instantly ready to debug without any special action.

Disadvantages of the debugger

As you have become painfully aware, the installation of the debugger leaves a lot to be desired. This debugger has not become very popular in the PostgreSQL community at large because of the rather large learning curve involved, and that's just to get it installed.

This form of debugging is meant for personal productivity while actively developing functions. It does not work well as an automation tool.

Summary

These debugging methods are designed to be used in cooperation with one another. They complement each other at different points in the development process. Where debugging using PL/pgSQL Debugger is highly effective while editing an existing (hopefully well written) function, other forms of debugging may be better suited to the quality assurance or automated data processing applications.

Because PL/pgSQL Debugger is meant to be a visual tool to work within `pgAdmin3`, it is possible that the developer may want to forego the visual debugger in the interest of some other feature.

7
Using Unrestricted Languages

You may have noticed that some of the PLs in PostgreSQL can be declared as untrusted. They all end in letter u to remind you that they are untrusted each time you use them to create a function.

This untrustedness brings up many questions:

- Does being untrusted mean that such languages are somehow inferior to trusted ones?
- Can I still write an important function in an untrusted language?
- Will they silently eat my data and corrupt the database?

The answers are no, yes, and maybe respectively. Let's discuss these questions in order.

Are untrusted languages inferior to trusted ones?

No, on the contrary, these languages are untrusted in the same way that a sharp knife is untrusted and should not be trusted to very small children, at least not without adult supervision. They have extra powers that ordinary SQL or even the trusted languages (such as PL/pgSQL) and trusted variants of the same language (PL/Perl versus PL/Perlu) don't have.

You can use the untrusted languages to directly read and write on the server's disks, and you can use it to open sockets and make Internet queries to the outside world. You can even send arbitrary signals to any process running on the database host. Generally, you can do anything the native language of the PL can do.

However, you probably should not trust arbitrary database users to have the right to define functions in these languages. Always think twice before giving *all privileges* on some untrusted language to a user or group by using the *u languages for important functions.

Can you use the untrusted languages for important functions? Absolutely. Sometimes, it may be the only way to accomplish some tasks from inside the server. Performing simple queries and computations should do nothing harmful to your database, and neither should connecting to the external world for sending e-mails, fetching web pages, or doing SOAP requests. They may cause delays and even queries that get stuck, but these can usually be dealt with by setting an upper limit as to how long a query can run by using an appropriate statement time-out value. Setting a reasonable statement time-out value by default is a good practice anyway.

So, if you don't deliberately do risky things, the probability of harming the database is no bigger than using a "trusted" (also known as "restricted") variant of the language. However, if you give the language to someone who starts changing bytes on the production database "to see what happens", you probably get what you asked for.

Will untrusted languages corrupt the database?

The power to corrupt the database is definitely there, since the functions run as the system user of the database server with full access to the filesystem. So, if you blindly start writing into the data files and deleting important logs, it is very likely that your database will be corrupted.

Additional types of denial-of-service attacks are also possible such as using up all memory or opening all IP ports; but there are ways to overload the database using plain SQL as well, so that part is not much different from the trusted database access with the ability to just run arbitrary queries.

So yes, you can corrupt the database, but please don't do it on a production server. If you do, you will be sorry.

Why untrusted?

PostgreSQL's ability to use an untrusted language is a powerful way to perform some nontraditional things from database functions. Creating these functions in a PL is an order of magnitude smaller task than writing an extension function in C. For example, a function to look up a hostname for an IP address is only a few lines in PL/Pythonu:

```
CREATE FUNCTION gethostbyname(hostname text)
  RETURNS inet
AS $$
  import socket
  return socket.gethostbyname(hostname)
$$ LANGUAGE plpythonu SECURITY DEFINER;
```

You can test it immediately after creating the function by using `psql`:

```
hannu=# select gethostbyname('www.postgresql.org');
 gethostbyname
----------------
 98.129.198.126
(1 row)
```

Creating the same function in the most untrusted language, C, involves writing tens of lines of boilerplate code, worrying about memory leaks, and all the other problems coming from writing code in a low-level language. While we will look at extending PostgreSQL in C in the next chapter, I recommend prototyping in some PL language if possible, and in an untrusted language if the function needs something that the restricted languages do not offer.

Why PL/Python?

All of these tasks could be done equally well using PL/Perlu or PL/Tclu; I chose PL/Pythonu mainly because Python is the language I am most comfortable with. This also translates to having written some PL/Python code, which I plan to discuss and share with you in this chapter.

Quick introduction to PL/Python

In the previous chapters, we discussed PL/pgSQL which is one of the standard procedural languages distributed with PostgreSQL. PL/pgSQL is a language unique to PostgreSQL and was designed to add blocks of computation and SQL inside the database. While it has grown in its breath of functionality, it still lacks the completeness of syntax of a full programming language. PL/Python allows your database functions to be written in Python with all the depth and maturity of writing a Python code outside the database.

A minimal PL/Python function

Let's start from the very beginning (again):

```
CREATE FUNCTION hello(name text)
  RETURNS text
AS $$
    return 'hello %s !' %  name
$$ LANGUAGE plpythonu;
```

Here, we see that creating the function starts by defining it as any other PostgreSQL function with a RETURNS definition of a text field:

```
CREATE FUNCTION hello(name text)
  RETURNS text
```

The difference from what we have seen before is that the language part is specifying plpythonu (the language ID for PL/Pythonu language):

```
$$ LANGUAGE plpythonu;
```

Inside the function body it is very much a normal python function, returning a value obtained by the name passed as an argument formatted into a string `'hello %s !'` using the standard Python formatting operator %:

```
    return 'hello %s !' %  name
```

Finally, let's test how this works:

```
hannu=# select hello('world');
     hello
---------------
 hello world !
(1 row)
```

And yes, it returns exactly what is expected!

Data type conversions

The first and last things happening when a PL function is called by PostgreSQL are converting argument values between the PostgreSQL and PL types. The PostgreSQL types need to be converted to the PL types on entering the function, and then the return value needs to be converted back into the PostgreSQL type.

Except for PL/pgSQL, which uses PostgreSQL's own native types in computations, the PLs are based on existing languages with their own understanding of what types (integer, string, date, …) are, how they should behave, and how they are represented internally. They are mostly similar to PostgreSQL's understanding but quite often are not exactly the same. PL/Python converts data from PostgreSQL type to Python types as shown in the following table:

PostgreSQL	Python 2	Python 3	Comments
`int2`, `int4`	`int`	`int`	
`int8`	`long`	`int`	
`real`, `double`, `numeric`	`float`	`float`	This may lose precision for numeric values
`bytea`	`str`	`bytes`	No encoding conversion is done, nor should any encoding be assumed.
`text`, `char()`, `varchar()`, and other text types	`str`	`str`	On Python 2, the string will be in server encoding. On Python 3, it is an unicode string.
All other types	`str`	`str`	PostgreSQL's `type` output function is used to convert to this string.

Inside the function, all computation is done using Python types and the return value is converted back to PostgreSQL using the following rules (this is a direct quote from official PL/Python documentation at `http://www.postgresql.org/docs/current/static/plpython-data.html`):

- When the PostgreSQL return type is Boolean, the return value will be evaluated for truth according to the Python rules. That is, `0` and empty string are `false`, but notably `f` is `true`.

- When the PostgreSQL return type is `bytea`, the return value will be converted to a string (Python 2) or bytes (Python 3) using the respective Python built-ins, with the result being converted `bytea`.

- For all other PostgreSQL return types, the returned Python value is converted to a string using Python's built-in `str`, and the result is passed to the input function of the PostgreSQL data type.

Strings in Python 2 are required to be in the PostgreSQL server encoding when they are passed to PostgreSQL. Strings that are not valid in the current server encoding will raise an error; but not all encoding mismatches can be detected, so garbage data can still result when this is not done correctly. Unicode strings are converted to the correct encoding automatically, so it can be safer and more convenient to use those. In Python 3, all strings are Unicode strings.

In other words, anything but 0, `False`, and an empty sequence, including empty string ` ` or dictionary becomes PostgreSQL `false`.

One notable exception to this is that the check for `None` is done before any other conversions and even for Booleans, `None` is always converted to `NULL` and not to the Boolean value `false`.

For the `bytea` type, the PostgreSQL byte array, the conversion from Python's string representation, is an exact copy with no encoding or other conversions applied.

Writing simple functions in PL/Python

Writing functions in PL/Python is not much different in principle from writing functions in PL/pgSQL. You still have the exact same syntax around the function body in $$, and the argument name, types, and returns all mean the same thing regardless of the exact PL/language used.

A simple function

So a simple `add_one()` function in PL/Python looks like this:

```
CREATE FUNCTION add_one(i int)
  RETURNS int AS $$
return i + 1;
$$ LANGUAGE plpythonu;
```

It can't get much simpler than that, can it?

What you see here is that the PL/Python arguments are passed to the Python code after converting them to appropriate types, and the result is passed back and converted to the appropriate PostgreSQL type for the return value.

Functions returning a record

To return a record from a Python function, you can use:

- A sequence or list of values in the same order as the fields in the return record

- A dictionary with keys matching the fields in the return record

- A class or type instance with attributes matching the fields in the return record

Here are samples of the three ways to return a record.

First, using an instance:

```
CREATE OR REPLACE FUNCTION userinfo(
                  INOUT username name,
                  OUT user_id oid,
                  OUT is_superuser boolean)
AS $$
   class PGUser:
       def __init__(self,username,user_id,is_superuser):
           self.username = username
           self.user_id = user_id
           self.is_superuser = is_superuser
   u = plpy.execute("""\
           select usename,usesysid,usesuper
             from pg_user
            where usename = '%s'""" % username)[0]
   user = PGUser(u['usename'], u['usesysid'], u['usesuper'])
   return user
$$ LANGUAGE plpythonu;
```

Then, a little simpler one using a dictionary:

```
CREATE OR REPLACE FUNCTION userinfo(
                  INOUT username name,
                  OUT user_id oid,
                  OUT is_superuser boolean)
AS $$
   u = plpy.execute("""\
           select usename,usesysid,usesuper
             from pg_user
            where usename = '%s'""" % username)[0]
   return {'username':u['usename'], 'user_id':u['usesysid'], 'is_
superuser':u['usesuper']}
$$ LANGUAGE plpythonu;
```

Finally, using a tuple:

```
CREATE OR REPLACE FUNCTION userinfo(
                    INOUT username name,
                    OUT user_id oid,
                    OUT is_superuser boolean)
AS $$
    u = plpy.execute("""\
            select usename,usesysid,usesuper
              from pg_user
             where usename = '%s'""" % username)[0]
    return (u['usename'], u['usesysid'], u['usesuper'])
$$ LANGUAGE plpythonu;
```

Notice [0] at the end of u = plpy.execute(...)[0] in all the examples. It is there to extract the first row of the result, as even for one-row results plpy.execute still returns a list of results.

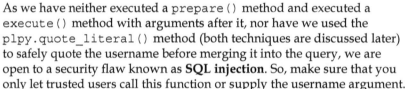

Danger of SQL injection!

As we have neither executed a prepare() method and executed a execute() method with arguments after it, nor have we used the plpy.quote_literal() method (both techniques are discussed later) to safely quote the username before merging it into the query, we are open to a security flaw known as **SQL injection**. So, make sure that you only let trusted users call this function or supply the username argument.

Calling the function defined via any of these three CREATE commands will look exactly the same:

```
hannu=# select * from userinfo('postgres');
 username | user_id | is_superuser
----------+---------+--------------
 postgres |      10 | t
(1 row)
```

It usually does not make sense to declare a class inside a function just to return a record value. This possibility is included mostly for cases where you already have a suitable class with a set of attributes matching the ones the function returns.

Table functions

When returning a set from a PL/Python functions, you have three options:

- Return a list or any other sequence of return type
- Return an iterator or generator
- `yield` the return values from a loop

Here, we have three ways to generate all even numbers up to the argument value using these different styles.

First, returning a list of integers:

```
CREATE FUNCTION even_numbers_from_list(up_to int)
  RETURNS SETOF int
AS $$
    return range(0,up_to,2)
$$ LANGUAGE plpythonu;
```

The list here is returned by a built-in Python function called range, which returns a result of all even numbers below the argument. This gets returned as a table of integers, one integer per row from the PostgreSQL function. If the RETURNS clause of the function definition would say int[] instead of SETOF int, the same function would return a single number of even integers as a PostgreSQL array.

The next function returns a similar result using a generator and returning both the even number and the odd one following it. Also, notice the different PostgreSQL syntax RETURNS TABLE(...) used this time for defining the return set:

```
CREATE FUNCTION even_numbers_from_generator(up_to int)
  RETURNS TABLE (even int, odd int)
AS $$
    return ((i,i+1) for i in xrange(0,up_to,2))
$$ LANGUAGE plpythonu;
```

The generator is constructed using a generator expression (x for x in <seq>). Finally, the function is defined using a generator using and explicit `yield` syntax, and yet another PostgreSQL syntax is used for returning SETOF RECORD with the record structure defined this time by OUT parameters:

```
CREATE FUNCTION even_numbers_with_yield(up_to int,
                                        OUT even int,
                                        OUT odd int)
  RETURNS SETOF RECORD
AS $$
    for i in xrange(0,up_to,2):
        yield i, i+1
$$ LANGUAGE plpythonu;
```

The important part here is that you can use any of the preceding ways to define a PL/Python set returning function, and they all work the same. Also, you are free to return a mixture of different types for each row of the set:

```
CREATE FUNCTION birthdates(OUT name text, OUT birthdate date)
  RETURNS SETOF RECORD
AS $$
    return (
        {'name': 'bob', 'birthdate': '1980-10-10'},
        {'name': 'mary', 'birthdate': '1983-02-17'},
        ['jill', '2010-01-15'],
    )
$$ LANGUAGE plpythonu;
```

This yields result as follows:

```
hannu=# select * from birthdates();
 name | birthdate
------+------------
 bob  | 1980-10-10
 mary | 1983-02-17
 jill | 2010-01-15
(3 rows)
```

As you see, the data returning a part of PL/Pythonu is much more flexible than returning data from a function written in PL/pgSQL.

Running queries in the database

If you have ever accessed a database in Python, you know that most database adapters conform to a somewhat loose standard called **Python Database API Specification v2.0** or **DBAPI 2** for short.

The first thing you need to know about database access in PL/Python is that in-database queries *do not* follow this API.

Running simple queries

Instead of using the standard API, there are just three functions for doing all database access. There are two variants: `plpy.execute()` for running a query, and `plpy.prepare()` for turning query text into a query plan or a prepared query.

The simplest way to do a query is with:

```
res = plpy.execute(<query text>, [<row count>])
```

This takes a textual query and an optional row count, and returns a result object, which emulates a list of dictionaries, one dictionary per row.

As an example, if you want to access a field `'name'` of the third row of the result, you use:

```
res[2]['name']
```

The index is 2 and not 3 because Python lists are indexed starting from 0, so the first row is `res[0]`, the second row `res[1]`, and so on.

Using prepared queries

In an ideal world this would be all that is needed, but `plpy.execute(query, cnt)` has two shortcomings:

- It does not support parameters
- The plan for the query is not saved, requiring the query text to be parsed and run through the optimizer at each invocation

We will show a way to properly construct a query string later, but for most uses simple case parameter passing is enough. So, the `execute(query, [maxrows])` call becomes a set of two statements:

```
plan = plpy.prepare(<query text>, <list of argument types>)
res = plpy.execute(plan, <list of values>, [<row count>])For example,
to query if a user 'postgres' is a superuser, use the following:
plan = plpy.prepare("select usesuper from pg_user where  usename =
$1", ["text"])
res = plpy.execute(plan, ["postgres"])
print res[0]["usesuper"]
```

The first statement prepares the query, which parses the query string into a query tree, optimizes this tree to produce the best query plan available, and returns the `prepared_query` object. The second row uses the prepared plan to query for a specific user's `superuser` status.

The prepared plan can be used multiple times, so that you could continue to see if user bob is `superuser`.

```
res = plpy.execute(plan, ["bob"])
print res[0]["usesuper"]
```

Caching prepared queries

Preparing the query can be quite an expensive step, especially for more complex queries where the optimizer has to choose from a rather large set of possible plans; so, it makes sense to re-use results of this step if possible.

The current implementation of PL/Python does not automatically cache query plans (prepared queries), but you can do it easily yourself.

```
try:
    plan = SD['is_super_qplan']
except:
    SD['is_super_qplan'] = plpy.prepare("....
    plan = SD['is_super_qplan']
<the rest of the function>
```

The values in SD[] and GD[] only live inside a single database session, so it only makes sense to do the caching in case you have long-lived connections.

Writing trigger functions in PL/Python

As with other PLs, PL/Pythonu can be used to write trigger functions. The declaration of a trigger function is different from an ordinary function by the return type RETURNS TRIGGER. So, a simple trigger function that just notifies the caller that it is indeed called looks like this:

```
CREATE OR REPLACE FUNCTION notify_on_call()
  RETURNS TRIGGER
AS $$
plpy.notice('I was called!')
$$ LANGUAGE plpythonu;
```

After creating this function, the trigger can be tested on a table using a trigger function:

```
hannu=# CREATE TABLE ttable(id int);
CREATE TABLE
hannu=# CREATE TRIGGER ttable_notify BEFORE INSERT ON ttable EXECUTE
PROCEDURE notify_on_call();
CREATE TRIGGER
hannu=# INSERT INTO ttable VALUES(1);
NOTICE:  I was called!
CONTEXT:  PL/Python function "notify_on_call"
INSERT 0 1
```

Of course, the preceding trigger function is quite useless, as will be any trigger without knowing when and on what data change the trigger was called. All the data needed by a trigger when it is called is passed in via the **trigger dictionary**, called **TD**. In TD, you have the following values:

Key	Value
TD["event"]	The event the trigger function is called for; one of the following strings is contained as the event: INSERT, UPDATE, DELETE, or TRUNCATE
TD["when"]	One of BEFORE, AFTER, or INSTEAD OF.
TD["level"]	ROW or STATEMENT.
TD["old"]	This is the before-command image of the row. For low-level UPDATE and DELETE triggers, this contains a dictionary for the values of the triggering row before the changes have been made by the command. It is None for other cases.
TD["new"]	This is the after-command image of the row. For low-level INSERT and UPDATE triggers, this contains a dictionary for the values of the triggering row after the changes have been made by the command. It is None for other cases. If you are in a BEFORE or INSTEAD OF trigger, you can make changes to this dictionary and then signal PostgreSQL to use the changed tuple by returning the string MODIFY from the trigger function.
TD["name"]	The trigger name from the CREATE TRIGGER command.
TD["table_name"]	The name of the table on which the trigger occurred.
TD["table_schema"]	The schema of the table on which the trigger occurred.
TD["relid"]	The **object identifier** (OID) of the table on which the trigger occurred.
TD["args"]	If the CREATE TRIGGER command included arguments, they are available from TD["args"][0] to TD["args"][n-1].

In addition to doing anything you can do in ordinary PL/Python functions, such as modifying data in tables, writing to files and sockets, and sending e-mails, you can also affect the behavior of the triggering command.

If TD["when"] is ("BEFORE", "INSTEAD OF") and TD["level"] == "ROW", you can return SKIP to abort the event. Returning None or OK indicates that the row is unmodified and it is OK to continue. Returning None is also the default behavior for Python if the function does a simple return or runs to the end without a return statement; so, you don't need to do anything for this case.

In case you have modified values in the `TD["new"]` and you want PostgreSQL to continue with the new values, you can return `MODIFY` to indicate that you've modified the new row. This can be done if `TD["event"]` is `INSERT` or `UPDATE`, otherwise the return value is ignored.

Exploring the inputs of a trigger

The following trigger function is useful when developing triggers, so that you can easily see what the trigger function is really getting when called:

```
CREATE OR REPLACE FUNCTION explore_trigger()
  RETURNS TRIGGER
AS $$
import pprint
nice_data = pprint.pformat(
  (
    ('TD["table_schema"]' , TD["table_schema"] ),
    ('TD["event"]'        , TD["event"] ),
    ('TD["when"]'         , TD["when"] ),
    ('TD["level"]'        , TD["level"] ),
    ('TD["old"]'          , TD["old"] ),
    ('TD["new"]'          , TD["new"] ),
    ('TD["name"]'         , TD["name"] ),
    ('TD["table_name"]'   , TD["table_name"] ),
    ('TD["relid"]'        , TD["relid"] ),
    ('TD["args"]'         , TD["args"] ),
  )
)
plpy.notice('explore_trigger:\n' + nice_data)
$$ LANGUAGE plpythonu;
```

This function formats all the data passed to the trigger in TD using `pprint.pformat`, and then sends it to the client as a standard Python info message using `plpy.notify`. For testing this out, we create a simple table and then put an `AFTER ... FOR EACH ROW ...` trigger using this function on that table:

```
CREATE TABLE test(
    id serial PRIMARY KEY,
    data text,
    ts timestamp DEFAULT clock_timestamp()
);

CREATE TRIGGER test_explore_trigger
 AFTER INSERT OR UPDATE OR DELETE ON test
   FOR EACH ROW
EXECUTE PROCEDURE explore_trigger('one', 2, null);
```

Now, we can explore what the trigger function actually gets:

```
hannu=# INSERT INTO test(id,data) VALUES(1, 'firstrowdata');
NOTICE:  explore_trigger:
(('TD["table_schema"]', 'public'),
 ('TD["event"]', 'INSERT'),
 ('TD["when"]', 'AFTER'),
 ('TD["level"]', 'ROW'),
 ('TD["old"]', None),
 ('TD["new"]',
  {'data': 'firstrowdata', 'id': 1, 'ts': '2013-05-13
12:04:03.676314'}),
 ('TD["name"]', 'test_explore_trigger'),
 ('TD["table_name"]', 'test'),
 ('TD["relid"]', '35163'),
 ('TD["args"]', ['one', '2', 'null']))
CONTEXT:  PL/Python function "explore_trigger"
INSERT 0 1
```

Most of this is expected and corresponds well to the table of TD dictionary values given in the previous table. What may be a little unexpected is the fact that the arguments given in the CREATE TRIGGER statement are all converted to strings, even the NULL. When developing your own triggers, either in PL/Python or any other language, it may be useful to put this trigger on the table as well to check that the inputs to the trigger are as expected. For example, it is easy to see that if you omit the FOR EACH ROW part, the TD['old'] and TD['new'] will be both empty as the trigger definition defaults to FOR EACH STATEMENT.

A log trigger

Now, we can put this knowledge to work and write a trigger that logs changes to the table to either a file or to a special log-collector process over UDP. Logging to a file is the simplest way to permanently log the changes in transactions which were rolled back. If these were logged to a log table, the ROLLBACK command would also remove the log records. This may be a crucial audit requirement for you business.

Of course, this also has the downside. You will be logging the changes that may not be permanent due to the transaction being rolled back, but this is the price you have to pay for not losing the log records.

```
CREATE OR REPLACE FUNCTION log_trigger()
RETURNS TRIGGER AS $$
    args = tuple(TD["args"])
    if not SD.has_key(args):
        protocol = args[0]
```

```
        if protocol == 'udp':
            import socket
            sock = socket.socket( socket.AF_INET,
                                  socket.SOCK_DGRAM )
            def logfunc(msg, addr=args[1],
                             port=int(args[2]), sock=sock):
                sock.sendto(msg, (addr, port))
        elif protocol == 'file':
            f = open(args[1], 'a+')
            def logfunc(msg,f=f):
                f.write(msg+'\n')
                f.flush()
        else:
            raise ValueError, 'bad logdest in CREATE TRIGGER'
        SD[args] = logfunc
        SD['env_plan'] = plpy.prepare("""
            select clock_timestamp(),
                   txid_current(),
                   current_user,
                   current_database()""", [])
    logfunc = SD[args]
    env_info_row = plpy.execute(SD['env_plan'])[0]
    import json
    log_msg = json.dumps(
        {'txid' : env_info_row['txid_current'],
         'time' : env_info_row['clock_timestamp'],
         'user' : env_info_row['current_user'],
         'db'   : env_info_row['current_database'],
         'table' : '%s.%s' % (TD['table_name'],
                              TD['table_schema']),
         'event' : TD['event'],
         'old' : TD['old'],
         'new' : TD['new'],
        }
    )
    logfunc(log_msg)
$$ LANGUAGE plpythonu;
```

First, this trigger checks if it already has a logger function defined and cached in the function's local dictionary SD[]. As the same trigger may be used with many different log destinations, the log function is stored under the key constructed as a Python tuple from the trigger function arguments in the CREATE TRIGGER statement. We can not use the TD["args"] list directly as a key, as Python dictionary keys have to be immutable, which a list is not, but a tuple is.

If the key is not present, meaning this is the first call to this particular trigger, we have to create an appropriate log function and store it. To do this, we examine the first argument for the log destination type.

For the `udp` log type, we create a UDP socket for writing. Then, we define a function, passing in this socket and also the other two trigger arguments as default arguments for the function. This is the most convenient way to create a closure, and to bundle a function with some data values in Python.

For the `file` type, we just open this file in the append mode (`a+`) and also create a log function. The log function writes a message to this file and flushes the write, so the data is written to the file immediately and not some time later when the write buffer fills up. The log function created in either of these cases is stored in `SD[tuple(TD["args"])]`.

At this point, we also prepare and save a query plan for getting other data we want to log and save this in `SD['env_plan']`. Now that we are done with the one-time preparations, we can proceed with the actual logging part, which is really very simple.

Next, we retrieve the logging function (`logfunc = SD[args]`) and get the row of the other logged data:

```
env_info_row = plpy.execute(SD['env_plan'])[0]
```

Finally, we convert all the logged data into one JSON object (`log_msg = json.dumps({...})`) and then use the logging function to send it to the log, `logfunc(log_msg)`.

And that's it.

Next, let's test it out to see how it works by adding another trigger to our test table we created earlier:

```
CREATE TRIGGER test_audit_trigger
  AFTER INSERT OR UPDATE OR DELETE ON test
    FOR EACH ROW
EXECUTE PROCEDURE log_trigger('file', '/tmp/test.json.log');
```

Any changes to the table done via `INSERT`, `UPDATE`, or `DELETE` are logged into `/tmp/test.json.log`. This file is initially owned by the same user running the server, usually postgres; so to look at it you need to either be that user or root user, or you have to change the permissions on the file created to allow reading.

If you want to test the UDP logging part, you just have to define another trigger with different arguments:

```
CREATE TRIGGER test_audit_trigger_udp
 AFTER INSERT OR UPDATE OR DELETE ON test
   FOR EACH ROW
EXECUTE PROCEDURE log_trigger('udp', 'localhost', 9999);
```

Of course, you need something to listen at the UDP port there. A minimalist UDP listener is provided for testing in `chapter07/logtrigger/log_udp_listener.py`. Just run it, and it prints any UDP packets received to `stdout`.

Constructing queries

PL/Python does a good job of managing values passed to prepared query plans, but a standard PostgreSQL query plan can take an argument in a very limited number of places. Sometimes, you may want to construct whole queries, not just pass values to predefined queries. For example, you can't have an argument for a table name, or a field name.

So, how would you proceed if you want to construct a query from the function's arguments and be sure that everything is quoted properly and no SQL injection would be possible? PL/Python provides three functions to help you with proper quoting of identifiers and data just for this purpose.

The function `plpy.quote_ident(name)` is meant for quoting identifiers, that is, anything that names a database object or its attribute like a table, a view, a field name, or function name. It surrounds the name with double quotes and takes care of properly escaping anything inside the string which would break the quoting:

```
hannu=# DO LANGUAGE plpythonu $$ plpy.notice(plpy.quote_ident(r'5"
\"')) $$;
NOTICE:  "5"" \"""
CONTEXT:  PL/Python anonymous code block
DO
```

And yes, `5" \"` is a legal table or field name in PostgreSQL; you just have to always quote it if you use it in any statement.

 The DO syntax creates an anonymous block inside your database session. It is a very handy way to run some procedural language code without needing to create a function.

The other two functions are for quoting literal values. The function, `plpy.quote_literal(litvalue)`, is for quoting strings and `plpy.quote_nullable(value_or_none)` is for quoting a value, which may be `None`. Both of these functions quote strings in a similar way, by enclosing them in single quotes (`str` becomes `'str'`) and doubling any single quotes or backslashes:

```
hannu=# DO LANGUAGE plpythonu $$ plpy.notice(plpy.quote_literal(r" \'
"))
$$;
NOTICE:  E' \\'' '
CONTEXT:  PL/Python anonymous code block
DO
```

The only difference between these two is that `plpy.quote_nullable()` can also take a value `None`, which will rendered as string `NULL` without any surrounding quotes. The argument to both of these has to be a string or a unicode string. If you want it to work with a value of any Python type, wrapping the value in `str(value)` usually works well.

Handling exceptions

With any bit of code, you need to make sure you handle when errors occur and your PL/Python functions are not an exception.

Before Version 9.1 of PostgreSQL, any error in an SQL query caused the surrounding transaction to be rolled back:

```
hannu=# DO LANGUAGE plpythonu $$
hannu$#   plpy.execute('insert into ttable values(1)')
hannu$#   plpy.execute('fail!')
hannu$# $$;
ERROR:  spiexceptions.SyntaxError: syntax error at or near "fail"
LINE 1: fail!
        ^
QUERY:  fail!
CONTEXT:  Traceback (most recent call last):
  PL/Python anonymous code block, line 3, in <module>
    plpy.execute('fail!')
PL/Python anonymous code block
```

You can manually use the SAVEPOINT attributes to control the boundaries of the rolled-back block, at least as far back as Version 8.4 of PostgreSQL. This will reduce the amount of the transaction that is rolled back:

```
CREATE OR REPLACE FUNCTION syntax_error_rollback_test()
  RETURNS void
AS $$
plpy.execute('insert into ttable values(1)')
try:
    plpy.execute('SAVEPOINT foo;')
    plpy.execute('insert into ttable values(2)')
    plpy.execute('fail!')
except:
    pass
plpy.execute('insert into ttable values(3)')
$$ LANGUAGE plpythonu;

hannu=# select syntax_error_rollback_test()
 syntax_error_rollback_test
----------------------------

(1 row)
```

When the SAVEPOINT foo; command is executed in PL/Python, an SQL error will not cause full "ROLLBACK;" but an equivalent of "ROLLBACK TO SAVEPOINT foo;", so only the effects of commands between SAVEPOINT and the error are rolled back:

```
hannu=# select * from ttable ;
 id
----
  1
  3
(2 rows)
```

In Version 9.1, there are two important changes in how PostgreSQL exceptions are handled. If no SAVEPOINT or subtransaction is used, each invocation of plpy. prepare() and plpy.execute() is run in it's own subtransaction, so that an error will only rollback this subtransaction and not all of the current transaction. Since using a separate subtransactions for each database interaction involves extra costs, and you may want to control the subtransaction boundaries anyway, a new Python context manager, plpy.subtransaction(), is provided.

For an explanation of Python's context managers, refer to `http://docs.python.org/library/stdtypes.html#context-manager-types` so that you can use the with statement in Python 2.6 or newer to wrap a group of database interactions in one subtransaction in a more Pythonic way:

```
hannu=# CREATE TABLE test_ex(i int);
CREATE TABLE
hannu=# DO LANGUAGE plpythonu $$
hannu$# plpy.execute('insert into test_ex values(1)')
hannu$# try:
hannu$#     with plpy.subtransaction():
hannu$#         plpy.execute('insert into test_ex values(2)')
hannu$#         plpy.execute('fail!')
hannu$# except plpy.spiexceptions.SyntaxError:
hannu$#     pass # silently ignore, avoid doing this in prod. code
hannu$# plpy.execute('insert into test_ex values(3)')
hannu$# $$;
DO
hannu=# select * from test_ex;
 i
---
 1
 3
(2 rows)
```

Atomicity in Python

While the subtransactions manage data changes in the PostgreSQL database, the variables on Python side's of the fence live their separate lives. Python does not provide even a single-statement level atomicity, as demonstrated by the following:

```
>>> a = 1
>>> a[1] = a = 2
Traceback (most recent call last):
  File "<stdin>", line 1, in <module>
TypeError: 'int' object does not support item assignment
>>> a
1
>>> a = a[1] = 2
Traceback (most recent call last):
  File "<stdin>", line 1, in <module>
TypeError: 'int' object does not support item assignment
>>> a
2
```

As you can see, it is possible that even a single multi-assignment statement can be executed only halfway through. This means that you have to be be prepared to fully manage your Python data yourself. The function, `plpy.subtransaction()`, won't help you in any way with managing Python variables.

Debugging PL/Python

First, let's start by stating that there is no debugger support when running functions in PL/Python; so it is a good idea to develop and debug a PL/Python function as a pure Python function as much as possible and only do the final integration in PL/Python. To help with this, you can have a similar environment in your Python development environment using the `plpy` module.

Just put the module in your path and do import `plpy` before you try running your prospective PL/Pythonu functions in an ordinary interpreter. If you use any of the `plpy.execute(...)` or `plpy.prepare()` functions, you also need to set up a database connection before using these by calling `plpy.connect(<connectstring>)`.

Using plpy.notice() for tracking the function's progress

The debugging technology I use most often in any language is printing out intermediate values as the function progresses. If the printout rolls past too fast, you can slow it down by sleeping a second or two after each print.

In standard python, this would look like this:

```
def fact(x):
    f = 1
    while (x > 0):
        f = f * x
        x = x - 1
        print 'f:%d, x:%d' % (f, x)
    return f
```

It will print out all intermediate values for f and x as it runs:

```
>>> fact(3)
f:3, x:2
f:6, x:1
f:6, x:0
6
```

If you try to use print in a PL/Python function, you will discover that nothing is printed. In fact, there is no single logical place to print to when running a pluggable language inside a PostgreSQL server.

The closest thing to print in PL/Python is the function `plpy.notice()`, which sends a PostgreSQL NOTICE to the client and also to the server log if `log_min_messages` is set to value `notice` or smaller.

```
CREATE FUNCTION fact(x int) RETURNS int
AS $$
    global x
    f = 1
    while (x > 0):
        f = f * x
        x = x - 1
        plpy.notice('f:%d, x:%d' % (f, x))
    return f
$$ LANGUAGE plpythonu;
```

Running this is much more verbose than the version with print, because each NOTICE also includes information about the CONTEXT from where the NOTICE comes:

```
hannu=# select fact(3);
NOTICE:   f:3, x:2
CONTEXT:  PL/Python function "fact"
NOTICE:   f:6, x:1
CONTEXT:  PL/Python function "fact"
NOTICE:   f:6, x:0
CONTEXT:  PL/Python function "fact"
 fact
------
    6
(1 row)
```

PL/Pythonu function arguments are passed in as globals

If you compared the `fact(x)` function in Python and PL/Python you noticed an extra line at the beginning of the PL/Python function:

```
global x
```

This is needed to overcome an implementation detail that often surprises PL/Pythonu developers; the function arguments are not the function arguments in the Python sense and neither are they locals. They are passed in as variables in the function's global scope.

Using assert

Similar to ordinary Python programming, you can also use Python's `assert` statement to catch conditions which should not happen:

```
CREATE OR REPLACE FUNCTION fact(x int)
  RETURNS int
AS $$
    global x
    assert x>=0, "argument must be a positive integer"
    f = 1
    while (x > 0):
        f = f * x
        x = x - 1
    return f
$$ LANGUAGE plpythonu;
```

To test this, call `fact()` with a negative number:

```
hannu=# select fact(-1);
ERROR:  AssertionError: argument must be a positive integer
CONTEXT:  Traceback (most recent call last):
  PL/Python function "fact", line 3, in <module>
    assert x>=0, "argument must be a positive integer"
PL/Python function "fact"
```

You will get a message about `AssertionError` together with the location of the failing line number.

Redirecting sys.stdout and sys.stderr

If all the code you need to debug is your own, the preceding two techniques will cover most of your needs. However, what do you do in cases where you use some third party libraries which print out debug information to `sys.stdout` and/or `sys.stderr`?

Well, in this case you can replace Python's `sys.stdout` and `sys.stdin` with your own pseudo file object that stores everything written there for later retrieval. Here is a pair of functions. The first of which does the capturing of `sys.stdout` or uncapturing; if it is called with the argument, `do_capture` set to `false`, and the second one returns everything captured:

```
CREATE OR REPLACE FUNCTION capture_stdout(do_capture bool)
  RETURNS text
AS $$
    import sys
    if do_capture:
```

```
        try:
            sys.stdout = GD['stdout_to_notice']
        except KeyError:
            class WriteAsNotice:
                def __init__(self, old_stdout):
                    self.old_stdout = old_stdout
                    self.printed = []
                def write(self, s):
                    self.printed.append(s)
                def read(self):
                    text = ''.join(self.printed)
                    self.printed = []
                    return text
            GD['stdout_to_notice'] = WriteAsNotice(sys.stdout)
            sys.stdout = GD['stdout_to_notice']
        return "sys.stdout captured"
    close:
        sys.stdout = SD['stdout_to_notice'].old_stdout
        return "restored original sys.stdout"
$$ LANGUAGE plpythonu;

CREATE OR REPLACE FUNCTION read_stdout()
  RETURNS text
AS $$
    return GD['stdout_to_notice'].read()
$$ LANGUAGE plpythonu;
```

Here is a sample session using the preceding functions:

```
hannu=# select capture_stdout(true);
   capture_stdout
--------------------
 sys.stdout captured
(1 row)

hannu=# DO LANGUAGE plpythonu $$
hannu$# print 'TESTING sys.stdout CAPTURING'
hannu$# import pprint
hannu$# pprint.pprint( {'a':[1,2,3], 'b':[4,5,6]} )
hannu$# $$;
DO
hannu=# select read_stdout();
         read_stdout
```

```
---------------------------------
TESTING sys.stdout CAPTURING    +
{'a': [1, 2, 3], 'b': [4, 5, 6]}+

(1 row)
```

Thinking out of the "SQL database server" box

We'll wrap up the chapter on PL/Python with a couple of sample PL/Pythonu functions for doing some things you would not usually consider doing inside the database function or trigger.

Generating thumbnails when saving images

Our first example uses Python's powerful **Python Imaging Library** (PIL) module to generate thumbnails of uploaded photos. For ease of interfacing with various client libraries, this program takes the incoming image data as a base-64 encoded string:

```
CREATE FUNCTION save_image_with_thumbnail(image64 text)
  RETURNS int
AS $$
import Image, cStringIO
size = (64,64) # thumbnail size

# convert base64 encoded text to binary image data
raw_image_data = image64.decode('base64')

# create a pseudo-file to read image from
infile = cStringIO.StringIO(raw_image_data)
pil_img = Image.open(infile)
pil_img.thumbnail(size, Image.ANTIALIAS)

# create a stream to write the thumbnail to
outfile = cStringIO.StringIO()
pil_img.save(outfile, 'JPEG')
raw_thumbnail = outfile.getvalue()

# store result into database and return row id
q = plpy.prepare('''
  INSERT INTO photos(image, thumbnail)
  VALUES ($1,$2)
```

```
        RETURNING id''', ('bytea', 'bytea'))
    res = plpy.execute(q, (raw_image_data,raw_thumbnail))

    # return column id of first row
    return res[0]['id']
    $$ LANGUAGE plpythonu;
```

The Python code is more or less a straight rewrite from the PIL tutorial, except that
the files to read the image from and write the thumbnail image to, are replaced with
Python's standard file-like `StringIO` objects. For all this to work, you need to have
PIL installed on your database server host.

In Debian/Ubuntu, this can be done by running `sudo apt.get install
python-imaging`. On most modern Linux distributions, an alternative is to use
Python's own package distribution system by running `sudo easy_install PIL`.

Sending an e-mail

The next sample is a function for sending e-mails from inside a database function:

```
CREATE OR REPLACE FUNCTION send_email(
    sender text,        -- sender e-mail
    recipients text,    -- comma-separated list of recipient addresses
    subject text,       -- email subject
    message text,       -- text of the message
    smtp_server text    -- SMTP server to use for sending
) RETURNS void
AS $$
    msg = "From: %s\r\nTo: %s\r\nSubject: %s\r\n\r\n%s" % \
        (sender, recipients, subject, message)
    recipients_list = [r.strip() for r
                                in recipients.split(',')]
    server = smtplib.SMTP(smtp_server)
    server.sendmail(sender_address, recipients_list, msg)
    server.quit()
$$ LANGUAGE plpythonu;
```

This function formats a message (`msg = ""`), converts a comma-separated **To:** address
into a list of e-mail addresses (`recipients_list = [r.strip()...]`), connects to a
SMTP server, and then passes the message to the SMTP server for delivery.

To use this function in a production system, it would probably require a bit more
checking on the formats and some extra error handling in case something goes
wrong. You can read more about Python's `smtplib` at `http://docs.python.org/
library/smtplib.html`.

Summary

In this chapter, we saw that it is relatively easy to do things way beyond what a simple SQL database server is supposed to support, thanks to its pluggable language's support.

In fact, you can do almost anything in the PostgreSQL server you could do in any other application server. Hopefully, this chapter just scratched the surface on some of the ideas of what you can do inside a PostgreSQL server.

In the next chapter, we will learn about writing PostgreSQL's more advanced functions in C. This will give you deeper access to PostgreSQL, allowing you to use a PostgreSQL server for even more powerful things.

8
Writing Advanced Functions in C

In the previous chapter, we introduced you to the possibilities of *untrusted* pluggable languages being available to a PostgreSQL developer to achieve things impossible in most other relational databases.

While using a pluggable scripting language is enough for a large class of problems, there are two main categories, where they may fall short, performance and depth of functionality. Most scripting languages are quite a bit slower than optimized C code when executing the same algorithms. For a single function, this may not be the case because common things such as dictionary lookups or string matching have been optimized so well over the years, but in general C code will be faster than scripted code. Also, in cases where the function is called millions of times per query, the overhead of actually calling the function and converting the arguments and return values to and from the scripting language counterparts can be a significant portion of the run time.

The second potential problem with pluggable languages is that most of them just do not support the full range of possibilities that is provided by PostgreSQL. There are just some things that simply cannot be coded in anything else but C. For example, when you define a completely new type for PostgreSQL, the type input and output functions which convert the type's text representation to internal representation and back need to handle PostgreSQL's pseudo-type cstring. This is basically the C string or a zero-terminated string. Returning cstring is simply not supported by any of the PL languages included in the core distribution, at least not as of PostgreSQL Version 9.2. The PL languages also do not support pseudo types ANYELEMENT, ANYARRAY, and specially "any" VARIADIC.

In the following sections, we will go step-by-step through writing some PostgreSQL extension functions in increasing complexity in C.

We will start from the simplest **add 2 arguments** function which is quite similar to the one in PostgreSQL manual, but we will present the material in a different order so setting up the build environment comes early enough so that you can follow us hands-on from the very beginning.

After that, we will describe some important things to be aware of when designing and writing code that runs inside the server — such as memory management, executing queries, and retrieving results.

As the topic of writing C-language PostgreSQL functions can be quite large and our space for this topic is limited, we will occasionally skip some of the details and refer you to the PostgreSQL manual for extra information, explanations, and specifications. We are also limiting this section to reference PostgreSQL 9.2. While most things will work perfectly fine across versions, there are references to paths that will be specific to a version.

Simplest C function – return (a + b)

Let's start with a simple function, which takes two integer arguments and returns the sum of these. We first present the source code and then will move on to show you how to compile it, load it into PostgreSQL, and then use it as any native function.

add_func.c

A C source file implementing `add(int, int) returns int` function looks like the following code snippet:

```
#include "postgres.h"
#include "fmgr.h"

PG_MODULE_MAGIC;

PG_FUNCTION_INFO_V1(add_ab);

Datum
add_ab(PG_FUNCTION_ARGS)
{
    int32   arg_a = PG_GETARG_INT32(0);
    int32   arg_b = PG_GETARG_INT32(1);

    PG_RETURN_INT32(arg_a + arg_b);
}
```

Let's go over the code explaining the use of each segment:

- `#include "postgres.h"`: This includes most of the basic definitions and declarations needed for writing any C code for running in PostgreSQL.

- `#include "fmgr.h"`: This includes the definitions for `PG_*` macros used in this code.

- `PG_MODULE_MAGIC;`: This is a "magic block" defined in `fmgr.h`. This block is used by the server to ensure that it does not load code compiled by a different version of PostgreSQL, potentially crashing the server. It was introduced in Version 8.2 of PostgreSQL. If you really need to write code which can also be compiled for PostgreSQL versions before 8.2 you need to put this between `#ifdef PG_MODULE_MAGIC` / `#endif`. You see this a lot in samples available on the Internet, but you probably will not need to do it for any new code. The latest pre-8.2 version became officially obsolete (that is unsupported) in November 2010, and even 8.2 community support ended in December 2011.

- `PG_FUNCTION_INFO_V1(add_ab);`: This introduces the function to PostgreSQL as Version 1 **calling convention** function. Without this line, it will be treated as an old-style Version 0 function. (See the information box following the Version 0 reference.)

- `Datum`: This is the return type of a C-language PostgreSQL function.

- `add_ab(PG_FUNCTION_ARGS)`: The function name is `add_ab` and the rest are its arguments. The `PG_FUNCTION_ARGS` definition can represent any number of arguments and has to be present, even for a function taking no arguments.

- `int32   arg_a = PG_GETARG_INT32(0);`: You need to use the `PG_GETARG_INT32(<argnr>)` macro (or corresponding `PG_GETARG_xxx(<argnr>)` for other argument types) to get the argument value.

- `int32   arg_b = PG_GETARG_INT32(1);`: Similar to the previous description.

- `PG_RETURN_INT32(arg_a + arg_b);`: Finally, you use the `PG_RETURN_<rettype>(<retvalue>)` macro to build and return a suitable return value.

You could also have written the whole function body as the following code:

```
PG_RETURN_INT32(PG_GETARG_INT32(0) + PG_GETARG_INT32(1));
```

But it is much more readable as written, and most likely a good optimizing C compiler will compile both into equivalently fast code.

Most compilers will issue a warning message as: `warning: no previous prototype for 'add_ab'` for the preceding code, so it is a good idea to also put a prototype for the function in the file:

```
Datum add_ab(PG_FUNCTION_ARGS);
```

The usual place to put it is just before the code line `PG_FUNCTION_INFO_V1(add_ab);`

While the prototype is not strictly required, it enables much cleaner compiles with no warnings.

Version 0 call conventions

There is an even simpler way to write PostgreSQL functions in C, called the **Version 0 Calling Conventions**. The preceding a + b function can be written as the following code:

```
int add_ab(int arg_a, int arg_b)
{
    return arg_a + arg_b;
}
```

Version 0 is shorter for very simple functions, but it is severely limited for most other usages — you can't do even some basic things such as checking if a pass by value argument *is null*, return a set of values, or write aggregate functions. Also, Version 0 does not automatically take care of hiding most differences of pass by value and pass by reference types which Version 1 does. Therefore, it is better to just write all your functions using Version 1 Calling Conventions and ignore the fact that Version 0 even exists.

From this point forward, we are only going to discuss Version 1 Calling Conventions for a C function.

In case you are interested, there is some more information on Version 0 at `http://www.postgresql.org/docs/current/static/xfunc-c.html#AEN50495`, in the section titled *35.9.3. Version 0 Calling Conventions*.

Makefile

The next step is compiling and linking the `.c` source file into a form that can be loaded into PostgreSQL server. This can all be done as a series of commands defined in a `Makefile` function.

The PostgreSQL manual has a complete section about what flags and included paths you should pass on each of the supported platforms and how to determine correct paths for including files and libraries.

Fortunately, all of this is also automated nicely for developers via the PostgreSQL Extension Building Infrastructure — or PGXS for short — which makes this really easy for most modules.

 Depending on which version of PostgreSQL you have installed, you may need to add the development package for your platform. These are usually the `-dev` or `-devel` packages.

Now, let's create our `Makefile` function. It will look like the following code:

```
MODULES = add_func

PG_CONFIG = pg_config
PGXS := $(shell $(PG_CONFIG) --pgxs)
include $(PGXS)
```

And you can compile and link the module by simply running `make`:

```
[add_func]$ make
gcc ... -c -o add_func.o add_func.c
gcc ... -o add_func.so add_func.o
rm add_func.o
```

Here the "..." stands for quite some amount of flags, includes, and libraries added by PGXS.

This produces a dynamically loadable module in the current directory which can be used directly by PostgreSQL if your server has access to this directory, which may be the case on a development server.

For a "standard" server, as installed by your package management system, you will need to put the module in a standard place. This can be done using the PGXS as well.

You simply execute `sudo make install` and everything will be copied to the right place; `[add_func]$ sudo make install`:

```
[sudo] password for hannu:
/bin/mkdir -p '/usr/lib/postgresql/9.2/lib'
/bin/sh /usr/lib/postgresql/9.2/lib/pgxs/src/makefiles/../../config/
install-sh -c -m 755  add_func.so '/usr/lib/postgresql/9.2/lib/'
```

CREATE FUNCTION add(int, int)

You are just one step away from being able to use this function in your database. You just need to introduce the module you just compiled to a PostgreSQL database using the CREATE FUNCTION statement.

If you followed the samples up to this point, the following statement is all that is needed, along with adjusting the path appropriately to where PostgreSQL is installed on your server.

```
hannu=# CREATE FUNCTION add(int, int)
hannu-#    RETURNS int
hannu-# AS '/usr/pgsql-9.2/lib/add_func', 'add_ab'
hannu-# LANGUAGE C STRICT;
CREATE FUNCTION
```

And voila—you have created your first PostgreSQL C-language extension function:

```
hannu=# select add(1,2);
 add
-----
   3
(1 row)
```

add_func.sql.in

While what we just covered is all that is needed to have a C function in your database, it is often more convenient to put the preceding CREATE FUNCTION statement in an SQL file.

You usually do not know the final path of where PostgreSQL is installed when writing the code, especially in the light of running on multiple versions of PostgreSQL and/or on multiple operation systems. Here also PGXS can help.

You need to write a file called add_funcs.sql.in as follows:

```
CREATE FUNCTION add(int, int) RETURNS int
    AS 'MODULE_PATHNAME', 'add_ab'
    LANGUAGE C STRICT;
```

And then add the following line in your Makefile function right after the MODULES= ... line:

```
DATA_built = add_func.sql
```

Now, when running `make`, the `add_funcs.sql.in` is compiled into a file `add_funcs.sql` with `MODULE_PATHNAME` replaced by the real path where the module will be installed.

```
[add_func]$ make
sed 's,MODULE_PATHNAME,$libdir/add_func,g' add_func.sql.in >add_func.sql
```

Also, `sudo make install` will copy the generated `.sql` file into the directory with other `.sql` files for extensions.

```
[add_func]$ sudo make install /usr/bin/mkdir -p '/usr/pgsql-9.2/share/
contrib'
/usr/bin/mkdir -p '/usr/pgsql-9.2/lib'
/bin/sh /usr/pgsql-9.2/lib/pgxs/src/makefiles/../../config/install-sh -c
-m 644  add_func.sql '/usr/pgsql-9.2/share/contrib/'
/bin/sh /usr/pgsql-9.2/lib/pgxs/src/makefiles/../../config/install-sh -c
-m 755  add_func.so '/usr/pgsql-9.2/lib/'
```

After this, the introduction of your C functions to a PostgreSQL database is as simple as `hannu=# \i /usr/pgsql-9.2/share/contrib/add_func.sql`.

CREATE FUNCTION

The path `/usr/pgsql-9.2/share/contrib/` to `add_func.sql` needs to be looked up from the output of the `make install` command.

> There is an even cleaner way to package up your code called Extensions where you don't need to look up for any paths and the preceding step would just be as follows:
>
> **CREATE EXTENSION chap8_add;**
>
> But it is relatively more complex to set up, so we are not explaining it here. We have a full chapter dedicated to Extensions later in this book.

Summary for writing a C function

Writing a C function used in PostgreSQL is a straightforward process.

1. Write the C code in `modulename.c`.
2. Write the SQL code for CREATE FUNCTION in `modulename.sql.in`.
3. Write a `Makefile` function.
4. Run `make` to compile a C file and generate `modulename.sql`.

5. Run `sudo make install` to install the generated files.

6. Run the generated `modulename.sql` in your target `databasehannu# \i /<path>/modulename.sql`.

Note that you must run the SQL code in any database you want to use your function. If you want all your new databases to have access to your newly generated function, add the function to your template database by running the `modulename.sql` file in database `template1` or any other database you are explicitly specifying in CREATE DATABASE command.

Adding functionality to add(int, int)

While our function works, it adds nothing in the preceding code just using SELECT A + B, but functions written in C are capable of so much more. Let's start adding some more functionality to our function.

Smart handling of NULL arguments

Notice the use of STRICT keyword in the CREATE FUNCTION add(int a, int b) in the previously mentioned code. This means that the function will not be called if any of the arguments are NULL, but instead NULL is returned straight away. This is similar to how most PostgreSQL operators works, including the + sign when adding two integers—if any of the arguments are NULL the complete result is NULL as well.

Next, we will extend our function to be smarter about NULL inputs and act like PostgreSQL's sum() aggregate function, which ignores NULL values in inputs and still produces sum of all non-null values.

For this, we need to do two things:

1. Make sure that the function is called when either of the arguments are NULL.

2. Handle NULL arguments by effectively converting a NULL argument to 0 and returning NULL only in cases where both arguments are null.

The first one is easy—just leave out the STRICT keyword when declaring the function. The latter one also seems easy as we just leave out STRICT and let the function execute. For a function with int arguments, this almost seems to do the trick. All NULL values show up as 0's and the only thing you miss will be returning NULL if both arguments are NULL.

Unfortunately, this only works by coincidence. It is not guaranteed to work in future versions, and even worse, if you do it the same way for pass by reference types it will cause PostgreSQL to crash on null pointer references.

Next we show how to do it properly. We need now to do two things: record if we have any non-null values and add all the non-null values we see:

```
Datum
add_ab_null(PG_FUNCTION_ARGS)
{
    int32   not_null = 0;
    int32   sum = 0;
    if (!PG_ARGISNULL(0)) {
        sum += PG_GETARG_INT32(0);
        not_null = 1;
    }
    if (!PG_ARGISNULL(1)) {
        sum += PG_GETARG_INT32(1);
        not_null = 1;
    }
    if (not_null) {
        PG_RETURN_INT32(sum);
    }
    PG_RETURN_NULL();
}
```

This indeed does what we need: hannu=# CREATE FUNCTION add(int, int) RETURNS int

```
    AS '$libdir/add_func', 'add_ab_null'

    LANGUAGE C;
CREATE FUNCTION
hannu=# SELECT add(NULL, NULL) as must_be_null, add(NULL, 1) as must_be_
one;
-[ RECORD 1 ]+--
must_be_null |
must_be_one  | 1
```

Achieving the same result using standard PostgreSQL statements, functions, and operators would be much more verbose: hannu=# SELECT (case when (a is null) and (b is null)

```
hannu(#              then null
hannu(#              else coalesce(a,0) + coalesce(b,0)
hannu(#          end)
hannu-# FROM (select 1::int as a, null::int as b)s;
-[ RECORD 1 ]
case | 1
```

In addition to restructuring the code, we also introduced two new macros
`PG_ARGISNULL(<argnr>)` for checking if argument `<argnr>` is NULL and
`PG_RETURN_NULL()` for returning NULL from a function.

> `PG_RETURN_NULL()` is different from `PG_RETURN_VOID()`.
> The latter is for using in functions which are declared to return
> pseudo-type `void` or in other words not to return anything.

Working with any number of arguments

After the rewrite to handle NULL values it seems that with just a little more effort, we
could make it work with any number of arguments. Just move the following code
inside the `for(;;)` cycle over the arguments and we are done:

```
if (!PG_ARGISNULL(<N>)) {
        sum += PG_GETARG_INT32(<N>);
        not_null = 1;
}
```

Actually, making the code use an array instead of simple type is not that simple
after all, and to make things more difficult there is no information or sample
code on how to work with arrays in official PostgreSQL manual for C-language
extension functions. The line between "supported" and "unsupported" when writing
C-language functions is quite blurred, and the programmer doing so is expected to
be able to figure some things out independently.

The bright side is that the friendly folks at the PostgreSQL mailing lists are usually
happy to help you out if they see that your question is a serious one and that you
have made some effort to figure out the basic stuff yourself.

To see how arguments of array types are handled, you have to start digging around
on the internet and/or in the backend code. One place where you can find a sample
is the `contrib/hstore/` module in the PostgreSQL source code. The `contrib`
modules are a great reference for examples of officially supported extension modules
from PostgreSQL.

Though the code there does not do exactly what we need – it works on `text[]` and
not `int[]` – it is close enough to figure out what is needed, by supplying the basic
structure of array handling and sample usage of some utility macros and functions.

After some digging around in back-end code and doing some web searches, it is not
very hard to come up with a code for integer arrays.

So here is C code for a function which sums all non-null elements in its argument array:

```c
#include "utils/array.h"  // array utility functions and macros
#include "catalog/pg_type.h" // for INT4OID

PG_MODULE_MAGIC;

Datum add_int32_array(PG_FUNCTION_ARGS);

PG_FUNCTION_INFO_V1(add_int32_array);

Datum
add_int32_array(PG_FUNCTION_ARGS)
{
    ArrayType   *input_array;

    int32   sum = 0;
    bool        not_null = false;
    // variables for "deconstructed" array
    Datum       *datums;
    bool        *nulls;
    int         count;
    // for for loop
    int         i;


    input_array = PG_GETARG_ARRAYTYPE_P(0);
    // check that we do indeed have a one-dimensional int array
    Assert(ARR_ELEMTYPE(input_array) == INT4OID);

    if (ARR_NDIM(input_array) > 1)
        ereport(ERROR,
                (errcode(ERRCODE_ARRAY_SUBSCRIPT_ERROR),
                 errmsg("1-dimensional array needed")));

    deconstruct_array(input_array,  // one-dimensional array
                    INT4OID,        // of integers
                    4,              // size of integer in bytes
                    true,           // int4 is pass-by value
                    'i',            // alignment type is 'i'
                    &datums, &nulls, &count); // result here

    for(i=0;i<count;i++) {
```

```
        // first check and ignore null elements
        if ( nulls[i] )
            continue;
        // accumulate and remember there were non-null values
        sum += DatumGetInt32(datums[i]);
        not_null = true;
    }

    if (not_null)
        PG_RETURN_INT32(sum);
    PG_RETURN_NULL();
}
```

So what new things are needed for handling array types as arguments? First, you
need to include definitions for array utility functions.

```
#include "utils/array.h"
```

Next, you need a pointer to your array.

```
ArrayType   *input_array;
```

Notice that there is no specific array-of-integers type but just a generic ArrayType,
which is used for any array.

To initialize the array from the first argument you use an already familiar
looking macro.

```
input_array = PG_GETARG_ARRAYTYPE_P(0);
```

Except that instead of returning a INT32 value it returns an array pointer
ARRAYTYPE_P.

After getting the array pointer, we perform a couple of checks.

```
Assert(ARR_ELEMTYPE(input_array) == INT4OID);
```

We assert that the element type of returned array is indeed an integer. (There are some
inconsistencies in PostgreSQL code as the plain integer type can be called either int32
or int4 depending on where the definition comes from, but they both do mean the
same thing, just one is based on the length in bits and the other in bytes.)

The type check is an assert and not plain runtime check because after you have your
SQL definition part of the function in place PostgreSQL itself takes care not to call the
function with any other type of array.

The second check is for checking that the argument is really a one-dimensional array (PostgreSQL arrays can have 1 to n dimensions and still be of the same type).

```
if (ARR_NDIM(input_array) > 1)
    ereport(ERROR,
            (errcode(ERRCODE_ARRAY_SUBSCRIPT_ERROR),
             errmsg("use only one-dimensional arrays!")));
```

If the input array has more than one dimension, we raise an error. (We will discuss PostgreSQL's error reporting in C later in its own section).

> If you need to work on arrays of arbitrary number of dimensions take a look at the source code of `unnest()` SQL function which turns any array into a set of array elements.
>
> The code is located in `backend/utils/adt/arrayfuncs.c` file in C function `array_unnest(...)`.

After we have done basic sanity checking on the argument, we are ready to start processing the array. As a PostgreSQL array can be quite a complex beast with multiple dimensions and array element starting at arbitrary index, it is easiest to use a ready-made utility function for most tasks. So here we use the `deconstruct_array(...)` function to extract a PostgreSQL array in three separate C variables:

```
Datum       *datums;
bool        *nulls;
int          count;
```

The `datums` pointer will be set to point to an array filled with actual elements. The `*nulls` will contain a pointer to an array of Booleans, which will be true if the corresponding array element was NULL, and `count` will be set to the number of elements found in the array.

```
deconstruct_array(input_array,  // one-dimensional array
                  INT4OID,      // of integers
                  4,            // size of integer in bytes
                  true,         // int4 is pass-by value
                  'i',          // alignment type is 'i'
                  &datums, &nulls, &count); // result here
```

The other arguments are as follows:

```
input_array - the pointer to PostgreSQL array
INT4OID - the type of array element
element size - the true in-memory size of the element type
is element pass-by-value
element alignment id
```

The type OID for int4 (=23) is already conveniently defined as INT4OID, the others you just have to look up.

The easiest way to get the values for type, size, passbyvalue, and alignment is to query these from the database.

```
c_samples=# select oid, typlen, typbyval, typalign from pg_type
c_samples-# where typname = 'int4';
-[ RECORD 1 ]
oid      | 23
typlen   | 4
typbyval | t
typalign | i
```

After the call to deconstruct_array(...) the rest is easy—just iterate over the value and null arrays and accumulate the sum:

```
for(i=0;i<count;i++) {
        // first check and ignore null elements
        if ( nulls[i] )
            continue;
        // accumulate and remember there were non-null values
        sum += DatumGetInt32(datums[i]);
        not_null = true;
    }
```

The only PostgreSQL-specific thing here is the use of the DatumGetInt32(<datum>) macro for converting the Datum to integer. The DatumGetInt32(<datum>) macro performs no checking of its argument to verify that it is indeed an integer (this is C remember, so no type info is available in data itself), but using the DatumGet*() macro helps us to make the compiler happy.

And we are done, as returning the sum (or NULL in case all elements were NULL values) is exactly the same as in our previous function.

While this is all from the C side, we still need to teach PostgreSQL about this new function. The simplest way is to declare a function which takes an int[] argument.

```
CREATE OR REPLACE FUNCTION add_arr(int[]) RETURNS int
    AS '$libdir/add_func', 'add_int32_array'
    LANGUAGE C STRICT;
```

It works fine for any integer array you pass it for:

```
hannu=# select add_arr('{1,2,3,4,5,6,7,8,9}');
-[ RECORD 1 ]
add_arr | 45
```

```
hannu=# select add_arr(ARRAY[1,2,NULL]);
-[ RECORD 1 ]
add_arr | 3
```

```
hannu=# select add_arr(ARRAY[NULL::int]);
-[ RECORD 1 ]
add_arr |
```

It even detects multidimensional arrays, and errors out if it is passed one: hannu=#
select add_arr('{{1,2,3},{4,5,6}}');

```
ERROR:  1-dimensional array needed
```

What if we want to use it the same way as our two-argument add(a,b) function?

Since Version 8.4 of PostgreSQL, it is possible using support for VARIADIC functions,
or functions taking a variable number of arguments.

Create the function as follows:

```
CREATE OR REPLACE FUNCTION add(VARIADIC a int[]) RETURNS int
    AS '$libdir/add_func', 'add_int32_array'
    LANGUAGE C  STRICT;
```

The previous calls to add_arr() can be rewritten as:

```
hannu=# select add(1,2,3,4,5,6,7,8,9);
-[ RECORD 1 ]
add | 45
```

```
hannu=# select add(NULL);
-[ RECORD 1 ]
add |
```

```
hannu=# select add(1,2,NULL);
-[ RECORD 1 ]
add | 3
```

Notice that you can't easily get the ERROR: 1-dimensional array needed as VARIADIC always constructs a one-dimensional array from the arguments.

The only thing missing is that you can't have PostgreSQL's function overloading mechanism to distinguish between add(a int[]) and add(VARIADIC a int[]) — you simply can't declare both of these at the same time because for PostgreSQL they are the same function with only the initial argument detection done differently. That is why the array version of the function was named add_arr. In case you need to call one VARIADIC function from another, there is a way. You can call the VARIADIC version with an argument of array type by prefixing the argument with VARIADIC on call side: hannu=# select add(ARRAY[1,2,NULL]);.

```
ERROR:  function add(integer[]) does not exist
LINE 1: select add(ARRAY[1,2,NULL]);
                   ^
```

```
HINT:  No function matches the given name and argument types. You might
need to add explicit type casts.
hannu=# select add(VARIADIC ARRAY[1,2,NULL]);
-[ RECORD 1 ]
add | 3
```

You can even smuggle in a multi-dimensional array: hannu=# select add(VARIADIC '{{1,2,3},{4,5,6}}');.

```
ERROR:  1-dimensional array needed
```

This calling convention also means that even when you create VARIADIC functions you need to check the array dimensions.

Basic guidelines for writing C code

After having written our first function, let's look at some of the basic coding guidelines for PostgreSQL backend coding.

Memory allocation

One of the places you have to be extra careful when writing C code in general is memory management. For any non-trivial C program you have to carefully design and implement your programs so that all your allocated memory is freed when you are done with it, or else you will "leak memory" and will probably run out of memory at some point.

As this is also a common concern for PostgreSQL it has it's own solution for it — Memory Contexts. Let's take a deeper dive into them.

Use palloc() and pfree()

Most PostgreSQL memory allocations are done using PostgreSQL's memory allocation function `palloc()` and not standard C `malloc()`. What makes `palloc()` special, is that it allocates the memory in current context and the whole memory is freed in one go when the context is destroyed. For example, the transaction context — which is the current context when a user-defined function is called — is destroyed and memory allocated is freed at the end of transaction. This means that most times the programmers do not need to worry about tracking `palloc()` allocated memory and freeing it.

It is also easy to create your own memory contexts if you have some memory allocation needs with different life spans. For example, the functions for returning a set of rows (described in more detail later in this chapter) have a structure passed to them, where one of the members is reserved for a pointer to a temporary context specifically for keeping a function-level memory context.

Zero-fill the structures

Always make sure that new structures are zero-filled, either by using `memset()` after allocating them or using `palloc0()`.

PostgreSQL sometimes relies on logically equivalent data items being also the same for bit-wise comparisons, and even when you set all the items in a structure it is possible that some alignment issues leave garbage in the areas between structure elements if any alignment padding was done by the compiler.

If you do not do this then PostgreSQLs hash indexes and hash joins may not work efficiently or even give wrong results. The planner's constant comparisons may also be wrong if constants which are logically the same are not the same via bit-wise equality, resulting in undesirable planning results.

Include files

Most of PostgreSQL internal types are declared in `postgres.h`, and the function manager interfaces (`PG_MODULE_MAGIC`, `PG_FUNCTION_INFO_V1`, `PG_FUNCTION_ARGS`, `PG_GETARG_<type>`, `PG_RETURN_<type>`, and so on) are in `fmgr.h`. Therefore, all your C extension modules need to include at least these two files. It is a good habit to include `postgres.h` first as it gives your code the best portability by (re)defining some platform dependent constants and macros. Including `postgres.h` also includes `utils/elog.h` and `utils/palloc.h` for you.

There are other useful include files in the utils/ subdirectory which you also may need to include like utils/array.h used in the last example.

Another often used include directory is catalog/ which gives you the initial (and by convention constant) part of most system tables so you do not need to look up things like type identifier for int4 data type, but can use its pre-defined value INT4OID directly. As of PostgreSQL 9.2, there are 79 constants for type IDs defined in catalog/pgtype.

The values in catalog/pg_* include files are always in sync with what gets put into the database catalogs by virtue of being *the* definition of the structure and contents of the system catalog tables. The .bki files used when initdb command sets up a new empty database cluster are generated from these .h files by genbki.pl script.

Public symbol names

It is the programmer's task to make sure that any symbol names visible in the .so files do not conflict with those already present in the PostgreSQL backend, including those used by other dynamically loaded libraries. You will have to rename your functions or variables if you get messages to this effect. This may be a bigger problem if the conflicts come from a third-party library your code is using, so test early in the development if you can link all the planned libraries to your PostgreSQL extension module.

Error reporting from C functions

One thing which went unexplained in the previous sample was the error reporting part:

```
if (ARR_NDIM(input_array) > 1)
    ereport(ERROR,
            (errcode(ERRCODE_ARRAY_SUBSCRIPT_ERROR),
            errmsg("use only one-dimensional arrays!")));
```

All error reporting and other off-channel messaging in PostgreSQL is done using the ereport(<errorlevel>, rest) macro. The main purpose of which is to make error reporting look like a function call.

The only parameter which is processed directly by `ereport()` is the first argument error level, or perhaps more exactly severity level or log level. All the other parameters are actually function calls which independently generate and store additional error information in the system to be written to logs and/or be sent to client. Being placed in the argument list of the `ereport()` makes sure that these other functions are called before the actual error is reported. This is important because in the case of an error level being ERROR, FATAL, or PANIC the system cleans up all current transaction state and anything after the `ereport()` call will never get a chance to run. Error states the end the transaction.

In case of ERROR the system is returned to a clean state and it will be ready to accept new commands.

Error level FATAL will clean up the backend and exit the current session.

PANIC is the most destructive one and it will not only end the current connection, but will also cause all other connections to be terminated. PANIC means that shared state (shared memory) is potentially corrupted and it is not safe to continue. It is used automatically for things like core dumps or other "hard" crashes.

"Error" states that are not errors

WARNING is the highest non-error level. It means that something may be wrong and needs user/administrator attention. It is a good practice to periodically scan system logs for warnings. Use this only for unexpected conditions. See the next one for things happening on regular basis. Warnings go to client and server logs by default.

NOTICE is for things which are likely of higher interest to users, like information about creating a primary key index or sequence for serial type (though these stopped to be NOTICE in the latest version of PostgreSQL). Like the previous one, NOTICE is sent both to client and server logs by default.

INFO is for things specifically requested by client, like VACUUM/ANALYSE VERBOSE. It is always sent to the client regardless of `client_min_messages` GUC setting, but is not written to a server log when using default settings.

LOG (and COMMERROR) are for servers operational messages, and by default are only written to the server log. The error level LOG can also be sent to client if `client_min_messages` is set appropriately, but COMMERROR never is.

There are DEBUG1 to DEBUG5 in increasing order of verbosity. They are specifically meant for reporting debugging info and are not really useful in most other cases, except perhaps for curiosity. Setting higher DEBUGx levels is not recommended in production servers, as the amount logged or reported can be really huge.

When are messages sent to the client

While most communication from server to client takes place after the command completes (or even after the transaction is committed in case of LISTEN/NOTIFY), everything emitted by ereport() is sent to the client immediately, thus the mention of *off-channel messaging* previously. This makes ereport() a useful tool for monitoring long-running commands such as VACUUM and also a simple debugging aid to print out useful debug info.

You can read a much more detailed description of error reporting at http://www. postgresql.org/docs/current/static/error-message-reporting.html.

Running queries and calling PostgreSQL functions

Our next stop is running SQL queries inside the database. When you want to run a query against the database, you need to use something called Server Programming Interface (or SPI for short). SPI gives programmer the ability to run SQL queries via a set of interface functions for using PostgreSQLs parser, planner, and executor.

> If the SQL you are running via SPI fails, the control is not returned to the caller, but instead the system reverts to a clean state via internal mechanisms for ROLLBACK. It is possible to catch SQL errors by establishing a *sub-transaction* around your calls. It is a bit involved process not yet officially declared "stable" and thus Therefore, it not present in the documentation on C extensions. If you need it, one good place to look at would be source code for various pluggable languages (pl/python, pl/proxy, ...) which do it and are likely to be maintained in good order if the interface changes.
>
> In PL/Python source, the functions to examine are in the plpython/plpy_spi.c file and are appropriately named Ply_spi_subtransaction_[begin|commit|abort]().

The SPI functions do return non-negative values for success, either directly via return value or in global variable SPI_result. Errors produce a negative value or Null.

Sample C function using SPI

Here is a sample function doing an SQL query via SPI_*() functions. It is a modified version of the sample form standard documentation (it uses *Version 1 Calling Conventions* and outputs a few more bit of information). The .c, .sql.in, and Makefile functions for this sample are available in the spi_samples/ subdirectory.

```
Datum
count_returned_rows(PG_FUNCTION_ARGS)
{
    char *command;
    int cnt;
    int ret;
    int proc;

    /* get arguments, convert command to C string */
    command = text_to_cstring(PG_GETARG_TEXT_P(0));
    cnt = PG_GETARG_INT32(1);

    /* open internal connection */
    SPI_connect();
    /* run the SQL command */
    ret = SPI_exec(command, cnt);
    /* save the number of rows */
    proc = SPI_processed;
    /* If some rows were fetched, print them via elog(INFO). */
    if (ret > 0 && SPI_tuptable != NULL)
    {
        TupleDesc tupdesc = SPI_tuptable->tupdesc;
        SPITupleTable *tuptable = SPI_tuptable;
        char buf[8192];
        int i, j;

        for (j = 0; j < proc; j++)
        {
            HeapTuple tuple = tuptable->vals[j];
            // construct a string representing the tuple
            for (i = 1, buf[0] = 0; i <= tupdesc->natts; i++)
                snprintf(buf + strlen (buf),
                        sizeof(buf) - strlen(buf),
                        " %s(%s::%s)%s",
                        SPI_fname(tupdesc, i),
                        SPI_getvalue(tuple, tupdesc, i),
                        SPI_gettype(tupdesc, i),
```

```
                           (i == tupdesc->natts) ? " " : " |");
                ereport(INFO, (errmsg("ROW: %s", buf)));
            }
        }

        SPI_finish();
        pfree(command);

        PG_RETURN_INT32(proc);
    }
```

After getting the arguments using the `PG_GETARG_*` macro, the first new thing shown is opening an internal connection via `SPI_connect()` which sets up the internal state for the following `SPI_*()` function calls. The next step is to execute a full SQL statement using `SPI_exec(command, cnt)`.

The `SPI_exec()` function is a convenience variant of `SPI_execute(...)` with `read_only` flag set to `false`. There is also a third version of execute at once SPI function, the `SPI_execute_with_args(...)` which prepares the query, binds the passed-in arguments, and executes in a single call.

After the query is executed, we save the `SPI_processed` value for returning the number of rows processed at the end of the function. In this sample, it is not strictly necessary, but in general you need to save any `SPI_*` global variable because they could be overwritten by the next `SPI_*(...)` call.

To show what was returned by the query and also to show how to access fields returned by SPI functions, we next print out detailed info any tuples returned by the query via `ereport(INFO, …)` call. We first checked that the `SPI_exec` call was successful (`ret > 0`) and that some tuples were returned (`SPI_tuptable != NULL`). and then for each returned tuple `for(j = 0; j < proc; ...)` we looped over the fields `for(i = 1; i <= tupdesc->natts; ...)` formatting the fields info into a buffer. We get the string representations of field name, value, and data type using SPI functions `SPI_fname()`, `SPI_getvalue()`, and `SPI_gettype()` and then send the row to user using `ereport(INFO, …)`. If you want to return the values from the function instead, see next sections on returning `SETOF` values and composite types.

Finally, we freed the SPI internal state using `SPI_finish();`. One can also free the space allocated for the command variable by `text_to_cstring(<textarg>)` function, though it is not strictly necessary thanks to the function call context being destroyed and memory allocated in it being freed anyway at the function exit.

Visibility of data changes

The visibility rules for data changes in PostgreSQL are that each command cannot see it's own changes but usually can see changes made by commands which were started before it, even when the command is started by the outer command or query.

The exception is when the query is executed with read-only flag set, in which case the changes made by outer commands are invisible to inner or called commands.

The visibility rules are described in the documentation at `http://www.postgresql.org/docs/current/static/spi-visibility.html` and may be quite complex to understand at first, but it may help to think of a read-only `SPI_execute()` call as being command-level, similar to transaction isolation level Serializable and read-write call as similar to Read-Committed isolation level.

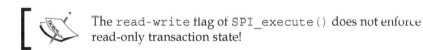

> The `read-write` flag of `SPI_execute()` does not enforce read-only transaction state!

There is more explanation at `http://www.postgresql.org/docs/current/static/spi-examples.html` in the *Sample session* section.

More info on SPI_* functions

There is a lot more information on specific `SPI_*()` functions in the official documentation.

For PostgreSQL Version 9.2 functions, `http://www.postgresql.org/docs/9.2/static/spi.html` is the starting point for the SPI docs.

More sample code is also available in the PostgreSQL source in regression tests at `src/test/regress/regress.c` and in the `contrib/spi/` module.

Handling records as arguments or returned values

As our next exercise, let's write a function which takes a record of three integers a, b, and c as an argument and returns a set of different record—all permutations of a, b, and c with an extra field x computed as $a*b+c$.

First, this function is written in PL/Python to make it easier to understand what we are trying to do: `hannu=# CREATE LANGUAGE plpythonu;`

```
CREATE LANGUAGE
hannu=# CREATE TYPE abc AS (a int, b int, c int);
CREATE TYPE
hannu=# CREATE OR REPLACE FUNCTION
hannu-#     reverse_permutations(r abc)
hannu-#   RETURNS TABLE(c int, b int, a int, x int)
hannu-# AS $$
hannu$#     a,b,c = r['a'], r['b'], r['c']
hannu$#     yield a,b,c,a*b+c
hannu$#     yield a,c,b,a*c+b
hannu$#     yield b,a,c,b*b+c
hannu$#     yield b,c,a,b*c+a
hannu$#     yield c,a,b,c*a+b
hannu$#     yield c,b,a,c*b+a
hannu$# $$ LANGUAGE plpythonu;
CREATE FUNCTION
hannu=# SELECT * FROM reverse_permutations(row(2,7,13));
-[ RECORD 1 ]
c | 2
b | 7
a | 13
x | 27
-[ RECORD 2 ]
c | 2
b | 13
a | 7
x | 33
-[ RECORD 3 ]
c | 7
b | 2
a | 13
x | 62
-[ RECORD 4 ]
c | 7
```

```
b |  13
a |  2
x |  93
-[ RECORD 5 ]
c |  13
b |  2
a |  7
x |  33
-[ RECORD 6 ]
c |  13
b |  7
a |  2
x |  93
```

There are three new things that we are going to touch in the following C implementation of similar function:

1. How to fetch an element of a RECORD passed as an argument?
2. How to construct a tuple to return a RECORD type?
3. How to return SETOF (a.k.a TABLE) of this RECORD?

So let's dive into the C code for this right away (a sample can be found in the chap8/c_records/ directory).

For clarity, we will explain this function in two parts, first doing a simple reverse(a,b,c) function, which returns just a single record of (c,b,a,x=c*b+a), and then expand it to return set of permutations such as the sample pl/pythonu function.

Returning a single tuple of a complex type

The first step in constructing a version of the reverse permutations function in C is to start with simply being able to return a single record of type abc.

```
Datum
c_reverse_tuple(PG_FUNCTION_ARGS)
{
    HeapTupleHeader th;
    int32   a,b,c;
    bool    aisnull, bisnull, cisnull;

    TupleDesc resultTupleDesc;
```

```
    Oid resultTypeId;
    Datum retvals[4];
    bool  retnulls[4];
    HeapTuple rettuple;

    // get the tuple header of 1st argument
    th = PG_GETARG_HEAPTUPLEHEADER(0);
    // get argument Datum's and convert them to int32
    a = DatumGetInt32(GetAttributeByName(th, "a", &aisnull));
    b = DatumGetInt32(GetAttributeByName(th, "b", &bisnull));
    c = DatumGetInt32(GetAttributeByName(th, "c", &cisnull));

   // debug: report the extracted field values
    ereport(INFO,
                (errmsg("arg: (a: %d,b: %d, c: %d)", a, b, c)) );

    // set up tuple descriptor for result info
    get_call_result_type(fcinfo, &resultTypeId, &resultTupleDesc);
    // check that SQL function definition is set up to return arecord
    Assert(resultTypeId == TYPEFUNC_COMPOSITE);
    // make the tuple descriptor known to postgres as valid return
type
    BlessTupleDesc(resultTupleDesc);

    retvals[0] = Int32GetDatum(c);
    retvals[1] = Int32GetDatum(b);
    retvals[2] = Int32GetDatum(a);
    retvals[3] = Int32GetDatum(retvals[0]*retvals[1]+retvals[2]);

    retnulls[0] = aisnull;
    retnulls[1] = bisnull;
    retnulls[2] = cisnull;
    retnulls[3] = aisnull || bisnull || cisnull;

    rettuple = heap_form_tuple( resultTupleDesc, retvals, retnulls );

    PG_RETURN_DATUM( HeapTupleGetDatum( rettuple ) );
}
```

Extracting fields from an argument tuple

Getting the fields of an argument tuple is easy. First, you fetch the `HeapTupleHeader` file of the argument into the `th` variable using the `PG_GETARG_HEAPTUPLEHEADER(0)` macro, and then for each field you get the `Datum` (a generic type which can hold any field value in PostgreSQL) by the field name using the `GetAttributeByName()` function and then assign its value to a local variable after converting it to `int32` via `DatumGetInt32()`.

```
a = DatumGetInt32(GetAttributeByName(th, "a", &aisnull));
```

The third argument to `GetAttributeByName(...)` is an address of a `bool` which is set to true if the field was `NULL`.

There is also a companion function `GetAttributeByNum()` if you prefer to get the attributes by their numbers instead of names.

Constructing a return tuple

Constructing the return tuple(s) is almost as easy.

First, you get the called functions return type descriptor using `get_call_result_type()` function.

```
get_call_result_type(fcinfo, &resultTypeId, &resultTupleDesc);
```

The first argument to this function is the `FunctionCallInfo` structure `fcinfo` which is used when calling the function you are currently writing (hidden behind the `PG_FUNCTION_ARGS` macro in the C function declaration), the other two arguments are addresses of the return type `Oid` and `TupleDesc` to receive the return tuple descriptor in case the function returns a record type.

Next, there is a safety assert for checking that the return type is really a record (or composite) type.

```
Assert(resultTypeId == TYPEFUNC_COMPOSITE);
```

This is to guard against errors in the `CREATE FUNCTION` declaration in SQL which tells PostgreSQL about this new function.

And there is still one thing before we construct the tuple.

```
BlessTupleDesc(resultTupleDesc);
```

The purpose of `BlessTupleDesc()` is to fill in the missing parts of the structure, which are not needed for internal operations on the tuple, but are essential when the tuple is returned from the function.

So we are done with the tuple descriptor and finally, we can construct the tuple or record itself to be returned.

The tuple is constructed using the `heap_form_tuple( resultTupleDesc, retvals, retnulls )`; function which uses the `TupleDesc` we just prepared. It also needs an array of `Datum` to be used as values in the return tuple, and an array of `bool`, which is used to determine if any field should be set to `NULL` instead of their corresponding `Datum` value. As all our fields are of type `int32` their values in `retvals` are set using `Int32GetDatum(<localvar>)`. The array `retnull` is a simple array of `bool` and needs no special tricks to set its values.

And finally we return the constructed tuple:

```
PG_RETURN_DATUM( HeapTupleGetDatum( rettuple ) );
```

Here, we first construct a `Datum` from the tuple we just constructed using `HeapTupleGetDatum()` and then use the `PG_RETURN_DATUM` macro.

Interlude – what is Datum

In this chapter, we use something called a `Datum` in several places. This calls for a bit of explanation about what a "`Datum`" is.

In short, a `Datum` is any data item the PostgreSQL processes and passes around. A `Datum` itself does not contain any type information or info about if the field is actually `NULL`. It is just a pointer to some memory. You always have to find out (or know beforehand) the type of any Datum you use and also how to find out if your data may be `NULL` instead of any real value.

In the preceding example, `GetAttributeByName(th, "b", &bisnull)` returns a Datum, and it can return something even when the field in the tuple is `NULL`, so always check for null-ness first. Also, the returned Datum itself cannot be used for much unless we convert it to some real type, as done in the next step using `DatumGetInt32()`, which simply converts the vague `Datum` to a real `int32` value, basically doing a cast form a memory location of an undefined type to `int32`.

The definition of `Datum` in `postgresql.h` is `typedef Datum *DatumPtr;` that is anything pointed to by a `DatumPtr`. Even though `DatumPtr` is defined as `typedef uintptr_t Datum;` it may be easier to think of it as a (slightly restricted) `void *`.

Once more, any real substance is added to a `Datum` by converting it to a real type.

You can also go the other way, turning almost anything into a `Datum` as seen at the end of the function:

```
HeapTupleGetDatum( rettuple )
```

Again, for anything else in PostgreSQL to make use of such Datum, the type information must be available somewhere else, in our case the return type definitions of the function.

Returning a set of records

Next, we modify our function to not just return a single record of re-ordered fields from argument record, but to return all possible orderings. We still add one extra field 'x' as an example of how you can use the values you extracted from the argument.

For set-returning functions, PostgreSQL has a special calling mechanism, where PostgreSQL's executor machinery will keep calling the function over and over again until it reports back that it does not have any more values to return. This return-and-continue behavior is very similar to how the yield keyword works in Python or JavaScript. All calls to the set returning function get an argument, a persistent structure maintained outside the function and made available to the function via macros: SRF_FIRSTCALL_INIT() for the first call and SRF_PERCALL_SETUP() for subsequent calls.

To make the example clearer, we provide a constant array of possible orderings to be used when permuting the values.

Also, we read argument fields a, b, and c only once at the beginning of the function and save the extracted values in a structure c_reverse_tuple_args, which we allocate and initialize at the first call. For the structure to survive through all calls, we allocate this structure in a special *memory context* which is maintained in the funcctx -> multi_call_memory_ctx and store the pointer to this structure in funcctx -> user_fctx. We also make use of funcctx fields: call_cntr and max_calls.

In the same code section run once at the first call, we also prepare the descriptor structure needed for returning the tuples. To do so, we fetch the return tuple descriptor by passing the address we get in funcctx->tuple_desc to function get_call_result_type(...), and we complete the preparation by calling BlessTuple(...) on it to fill in the missing bits needed for using it for returning values.

At the end of this section, we restore the memory context. While you usually do not need to pfree() the things you have palloc() allocated, you should always remember to restore the memory context when you are done using any context you have switched to or else you risk messing up PostgreSQL in a way that can be hard to debug later!

The rest is something that gets done at each call, including first one.

We start by checking that there is still something to do by comparing that current call to the max calls parameter. This is by no means the only way to determine if we have returned all values, but it is the simplest way if you know ahead how many rows you are going to return. If there are no more rows to return, we signal this back using SRF_RETURN_DONE().

The rest is very similar to what the previous single-tuple function did. We compute the retvals and retnulls arrays using the index permutations array ips and then construct a tuple to return using heap_form_tuple(funcctx->tuple_desc, retvals, retnulls);.

Finally, we return the tuple using macro SRF_RETURN_NEXT(...), converting the tuple to Datum, as this is what the macro expects.

One more thing to note, all current versions of PostgreSQL will always keep calling your function until it returns SRF_RETURN_DONE(). There is currently no way to do an "early exit" from the callers side. This means that if your function returns 1 million rows and you do.

```
select * from mymillionrowfunction() limit 3;
```

The function will get called 1 million times internally, and all the results will be cached, and only after this the first 3 rows will be returned and the remaining 999,997 rows are discarded. This is not a fundamental limitation, but just an implementation detail which is likely to change in some future version of PostgreSQL. Don't hold your breath though, this will only happen if somebody finds this valuable enough to implement.

The source with modifications described previously are as follows:

```
struct c_reverse_tuple_args {
    int32   argvals[3];
    bool    argnulls[3];
    bool    anyargnull;
};

Datum
c_permutations_x(PG_FUNCTION_ARGS)
{
    FuncCallContext    *funcctx;

    const char  *argnames[3] = {"a","b","c"};
    // 6 possible index permutations for 0,1,2
    const int   ips[6][3] = {{0,1,2},{0,2,1},
                             {1,0,2},{1,2,0},
                             {2,0,1},{2,1,0}};
```

```
    int i, call_nr;

    struct c_reverse_tuple_args* args;

    if(SRF_IS_FIRSTCALL())
    {
        HeapTupleHeader th = PG_GETARG_HEAPTUPLEHEADER(0);
        MemoryContext   oldcontext;
        /* create a function context for cross-call persistence */
        funcctx = SRF_FIRSTCALL_INIT();
        /* switch to memory context appropriate for multiple function
calls */
        oldcontext = MemoryContextSwitchTo(
                                                          funcctx-
>multi_call_memory_ctx

);
        /* allocate and zero-fill struct for persisting extracted
arguments*/
        args = palloc0(sizeof(struct c_reverse_tuple_args));
        args->anyargnull = false;
        funcctx->user_fctx = args;
        /* total number of tuples to be returned */
        funcctx->max_calls = 6; // there are 6 permutations of 3
elements
        // extract argument values and NULL-ness
        for(i=0;i<3;i++){
            args->argvals[i] = DatumGetInt32(GetAttributeByName(th,
argnames[i], &(args->argnulls[i])));
            if (args->argnulls[i])
                args->anyargnull = true;
        }
        // set up tuple for result info
        if (get_call_result_type(fcinfo, NULL, &funcctx->tuple_desc)
            != TYPEFUNC_COMPOSITE)
            ereport(ERROR,
                    (errcode(ERRCODE_FEATURE_NOT_SUPPORTED),
                     errmsg("function returning record called in
context "
                            "that cannot accept type record")));
        BlessTupleDesc(funcctx->tuple_desc);
        // restore memory context
```

```
            MemoryContextSwitchTo(oldcontext);
    }

    funcctx = SRF_PERCALL_SETUP();
    args = funcctx->user_fctx;
    call_nr = funcctx->call_cntr;

    if (call_nr < funcctx->max_calls) {
        HeapTuple    rettuple;
        Datum        retvals[4];
        bool         retnulls[4];

        for(i=0;i<3;i++){
            retvals[i] = Int32GetDatum(args->argvals[ips[call_nr]
[i]]);
            retnulls[i] = args->argnulls[ips[call_nr][i]];
        }
        retvals[3] = Int32GetDatum(args->argvals[ips[call_nr][0]]
                                                * args-
>argvals[ips[call_nr][1]]
                                                + args-
>argvals[ips[call_nr][2]]);
        retnulls[3] = args->anyargnull;

        rettuple = heap_form_tuple(funcctx->tuple_desc, retvals,
retnulls);

        SRF_RETURN_NEXT(funcctx, HeapTupleGetDatum( rettuple ));
    }
    else    /* do when there is no more left */
    {
        SRF_RETURN_DONE(funcctx);
    }

}
```

Fast capturing of database changes

Some obvious things to code in C are logging, or auditing triggers, which get called at each INSERT, UPDATE, or DELETE to a table. We have not set aside enough space in this book to explain everything needed for C triggers, but interested reader could look up the source code for the skytools package where you can find more than one way to write triggers in C.

The highly optimized C source for the two main triggers, `logtriga` and `logutriga`, includes everything you need to capture these changes to a table and even detecting table structure changes while the code is running.

The latest source code for `skytools` can be found at `http://pgfoundry.org/projects/skytools`.

Doing something at commit/rollback

As of this writing, there is no possibility to define a trigger function which is executed *ON COMMIT* or *ON ROLLBACK*. However, if you really need to have some code executed on these database events, you have a possibility to register a C-language function to be called on these events. Unfortunately, this registration cannot be done in a permanent way like triggers, but the registration function has to be called each time a new connection starts using.

```
RegisterXactCallback(my_xact_callback, NULL);
```

Use `grep -r RegisterXactCallback` in the `contrib/` directory of PostgreSQL's source code to find files with examples of actual callback functions.

Synchronizing between backends

All the preceding functions are designed to run in a single process/backend as if the other PostgreSQL processes did not exist.

But what if you want to log something to a single file from multiple backends?

Seems easy — just open the file and write what you want. Unfortunately, it is not that easy if you want to do it from multiple parallel processes and you do not overwrite or mix up the data with what other processes write.

To have more control over the writing order between backends, you need to have some kind of inter-process synchronization, and the easiest way to do this in PostgreSQL is to use *shared memory* and *light-weight locks* (`LWLocks`).

To allocate its own shared memory segment your `.so` file needs to be pre-loaded, that is, it should be one of the pre-load libraries given in `postgresql.conf` variable `shared_preload_libraries`.

In the `_PG_init()` function of your module, you ask for the address of a name shared memory segment. If you are the first one asking for the segment, you are also responsible for initializing the shared structures, including creating and storing any LWLocks you wish to use in your module.

Additional resources for C

In this chapter, we were able to only give you a very basic introduction to what is possible in C. Here is some advice on how to get more information.

First, there is of course the chapter *C-Language Functions* in the PostgreSQL manual. This can be found online at `http://www.postgresql.org/docs/current/static/xfunc-c.html` and as with most of the online PostgreSQL manual, you usually can get to older versions if they exist.

The next one, not surprisingly, is the PostgreSQL source code itself. However, you will usually not get very far by just opening the files or using `grep` to find what you need. If you are good with using `ctags` (`http://en.wikipedia.org/wiki/Ctags`) or other similar tool, it is definitely recommended.

Also, if you are new to these types of large-code exploration systems, then a really good resource for finding and examining PostgreSQL internals is maintained at `http://doxygen.postgresql.org/`. This points to the latest `git` master so it may not be accurate for your version of PostgreSQL, but it is usually good enough and at least provides a nice starting point for digging around in the source code of your version.

Quite often, you will find something to base (parts of) your C source on in the `contrib/` directory in the source code. To get an idea what is there, read through the *Appendix F, Additional Supplied Modules* (`http://www.postgresql.org/docs/current/static/contrib.html`). It may even be that somebody has already written what you need. There are even more modules in `http://pgfoundry.org` for you to examine and choose. A word of warning though, while modules in `contrib/` is checked at least by one or two competent PostgreSQL core programmers, the things at `pgfoundry` can be of wildly varying quality. The top active projects are really good however, so the main things to look at when determining if you can use them as learning source are how active the project is and when it was last updated.

There is also a set of GUC parameters specifically for development and debugging which are usually left out of sample `postgresql.conf` file. The descriptions and some explanation is available at `http://www.postgresql.org/docs/current/static/runtime-config-developer.html`.

Summary

As C is the language that PostgreSQL itself is written in, it is very hard to draw a distinction on what is an extension function using a defined API and what is hacking PostgreSQL itself.

Some of the topics that we did not touch at all were:

- Creating new installable types from scratch—see `contrib/hstore/` for a full implementation of a new type.

- Creating new index methods—download some older version of PosrgreSQL to see how full text indexing support was provided as an add-on.

- Implementing a new PL/* language—search for `pl/lolcode` for a language whose sole purpose is to demonstrate how a PotgreSQLs PL/* language should be written (see `http://pgfoundry.org/projects/pllolcode/`). You also may want to check out the source code for PL/Proxy for a clean and well maintained PL language. (The usage of PL/Proxy is described in the next chapter.)

Hopefully this chapter gave you enough info to at least start writing PostgreSQL extension functions in C.

If you need more than what is available here or in the official PostgreSQL documentation, then remember that lots of PostgreSQLs backend *developer* documentation—often including answers to the questions *How?* and *Why?* —is in the source files. And lot of that can be relevant also to C extensions.

So remember—Use The Source, Luke!

9
Scaling Your Database with PL/Proxy

If you have followed the advice in the previous chapters for doing all your database access through functions, you are in a great position to scale your database by "horizontally" distributing the data over multiple servers. Horizontal distribution means that you keep just a portion of a table on each "partition" database, and that you have a method to automatically access the right database when accessing the data.

We will gently introduce the concepts leading to the PL/Proxy partitioning language, and then delve into the syntax and proper usage of the language itself. Let's start with writing a scalable application from scratch. First, we will write it to be as highly performing as possible on one server. Then, we will scale it by spreading it out on several servers. We will first get this implemented in PL/Pythonu and then as samples done in the theme special language for this chapter—PL/Proxy.

 This approach is worth taking only if you have (plans for) a really large database. For most databases, one server plus one or perhaps two hot standby servers should be more than enough.

Simple single-server chat

Perhaps, the simplest application needing this kind of scalability is a messaging (or chat) application; so let's write one.

The initial single-server implementation has the following specifications:

- There should be users and messages.
- Each user has a username, password, e-mail, list of friends, and a flag to indicate if the user wants to get messages from only their friends, or from everybody.

- For users, there are methods for:
  - ° Registering new users
  - ° Updating the list of friends
  - ° Logging in

- Each message has a sender, receiver, message body, and timestamps for sending and reading the message.

- For messages, there are methods for:
  - ° Sending a message
  - ° Retrieving new messages

A minimalistic system implementing this could look like the following:

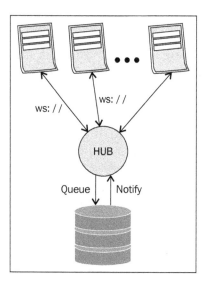

Here, a web page opens a WebSocket (ws://) to a HUB (a message concentrator) which in turn talks to a database. On each new connection, the HUB logs in and on successful login opens a WebSocket connection to the web page. It then sends all new messages that have accumulated for the logged-in user since the last time they retrieved their messages. After that, the HUB waits for new messages and pushes them to the web page as they arrive.

The database part has two tables, the `user_info` table:

```
CREATE TABLE user_info (
    username text primary key,
    pwdhash text not null,  -- base64 encoded md5 hash of password
    email text,
    friend_list text[], -- list of buddies usernames
    friends_only boolean not null default false
);
```

As well as the `message` table:

```
CREATE TABLE message (
    from_user text not null references user_info(username),
    sent_at timestamp not null default current_timestamp,
    to_user text not null references user_info(username),
    read_at timestamp, -- when was this retrieved by to_user
    msq_body text not null,
    delivery_status text not null default 'outgoing' --  ('sent',
"failed")
);
```

As this is still an "all-in-one database" implementation, the database functions corresponding to application methods are very simple.

Creating a user:

```
CREATE or REPLACE FUNCTION new_user(
    IN i_username text, IN i_pwdhash text, IN i_email text,
    OUT status int, OUT message text )
AS $$
BEGIN
    INSERT INTO user_info( username, pwdhash, email)
                VALUES ( i_username, i_pwdhash, i_email);
    status = 200;
    message = 'OK';
EXCEPTION WHEN unique_violation THEN
    status = 500;
    message = 'USER EXISTS';
END;
$$ LANGUAGE plpgsql SECURITY DEFINER;
```

This method just fails when the user is already defined. A more "real-life" function would propose a list of available usernames in this case.

The method for login returns status 500 for failure and 200 or 201 for success. 201 means that there are unread messages for this user:

```
CREATE OR REPLACE FUNCTION login(
    IN i_username text, IN i_pwdhash text,
    OUT status int, OUT message text )
AS $$
BEGIN
    PERFORM 1 FROM user_info
    WHERE ( username, pwdhash) = ( i_username, i_pwdhash);
    IF NOT FOUND THEN
        status = 500;
        message = 'NOT FOUND';
    END IF;
    PERFORM 1 FROM  message
    WHERE  to_user =  i_username
      AND  read_at IS NULL;
    IF FOUND THEN
        status = 201;
        message = 'OK. NEW MESSAGES';
    ELSE
        status = 200;
        message = 'OK. NO MESSAGES';
    END IF;
END;
$$ LANGUAGE plpgsql SECURITY DEFINER;
```

The other two user methods are for changing the friends list and telling the system whether they want to receive mails that are only from friends. Error checking is omitted here for brevity:

```
CREATE or REPLACE FUNCTION set_friends_list(
    IN i_username text, IN i_friends_list text[],
    OUT status int, OUT message text )
AS $$
BEGIN
    UPDATE user_info
       SET friend_list =  i_friends_list
    WHERE  username =  i_username;
    status = 200;
    message = 'OK';
END;
$$ LANGUAGE plpgsql SECURITY DEFINER;

CREATE or REPLACE FUNCTION msg_from_friends_only(
```

```
    IN i_username text, IN i_friends_only boolean,
        OUT status int, OUT message text )
    AS $$
    BEGIN
        UPDATE user_info SET  friends_only =   i_friends_only
        WHERE  username =  i_username;
        status = 200;
        message = 'OK';
    END;
    $$ LANGUAGE plpgsql SECURITY DEFINER;
```

The function used for messaging simply send messages is as follows:

```
CREATE or REPLACE FUNCTION send_message(
    IN i_from_user text, IN i_to_user text, IN i_message text,
    OUT status int, OUT message text )
AS $$
BEGIN
    PERFORM 1 FROM  user_info
    WHERE  username = i_to_user
      AND (NOT friends_only OR friend_list @> ARRAY[i_from_user]);
    IF NOT FOUND THEN
        status = 400;
        message = 'SENDING FAILED';
        RETURN;
    END IF;
    INSERT INTO message(from_user, to_user, msg_body, delivery_status)
    VALUES (i_from_user, i_to_user, i_message, 'sent');
    status = 200;
    message = 'OK';
EXCEPTION
    WHEN foreign_key_violation THEN
        status = 500;
        message = 'FAILED';
END;
$$ LANGUAGE plpgsql SECURITY DEFINER;
```

The function used for messaging simply get messages is as follows:

```
CREATE or REPLACE FUNCTION get_new_messages(
    IN i_username text,
    OUT o_status int, OUT o_message_text text,
    OUT o_from_user text, OUT o_sent_at timestamp)
RETURNS SETOF RECORD
AS $$
```

```
BEGIN
    FOR o_status,  o_message_text, o_from_user,  o_sent_at IN
        UPDATE message
        SET read_at = CURRENT_TIMESTAMP,
            delivery_status = 'read'
        WHERE to_user =  i_username AND read_at IS NULL
        RETURNING 200, msg_body, from_user , sent_at
    LOOP
        RETURN NEXT;
    END LOOP;
END;
$$ LANGUAGE plpgsql SECURITY DEFINER;
```

We are almost done with the database part of our simple server. To finish it up, we need to do some initial performance tuning, and for that we need some data in our tables. The easiest way is to use the `generate_series()` function to generate a list of numbers, which we will use as usernames. For our initial testing, names like 7 or 42 are as good as Bob, Mary, or Jill:

```
hannu=# SELECT new_user(generate_series::text, 'pwd', generate_
series::text || '@pg.org')
hannu-#    FROM generate_series(1,100000);


hannu=# WITH ns(n,len) AS (
hannu(#         SELECT *,(random() * 10)::int FROM generate_
series(1,100000))
hannu-#                 SELECT set_friends_list(ns.n::text,
hannu(#                    ARRAY( (SELECT (random() * 100000)::int
hannu(#                          FROM generate_series(1,len))
)::text[]
hannu(# )
hannu-# FROM ns ;




Now we have 100,000 users with 0 to 10 friends each, for a
total of 501,900 friends. hannu=# SELECT count(*) FROM (SELECT
username,unnest(friend_list) FROM user_info) a;
-[ RECORD 1 ]-
count | 501900
```

Now, let's send each of the friends a message:

```
hannu=# SELECT send_message(username,unnest(friend_list),'hello
friend!') FROM user_info;
```

Look how fast we can retrieve the messages:

```
hannu=# select get_new_messages('50000');
                        get_new_messages
----------------------------------------------------------
 (200,"hello friend!",49992,"2012-01-09 02:23:28.470979")
 (200,"hello friend!",49994,"2012-01-09 02:23:28.470979")
 (200,"hello friend!",49995,"2012-01-09 02:23:28.470979")
 (200,"hello friend!",49996,"2012-01-09 02:23:28.470979")
 (200,"hello friend!",49997,"2012-01-09 02:23:28.470979")
 (200,"hello friend!",49999,"2012-01-09 02:23:28.470979")
 (200,"hello friend!",50000,"2012-01-09 02:23:28.470979")
(7 rows)

Time: 763.513 ms
```

Spending almost a second getting seven messages seems slow, so we need to optimize a bit.

The first thing to do is to add indexes for retrieving the messages:

```
hannu=# CREATE INDEX message_from_user_ndx ON  message(from_user);
CREATE INDEX
Time: 4341.890 ms
hannu=# CREATE INDEX message_to_user_ndx ON  message(to_user);
CREATE INDEX
Time: 4340.841 ms
```

And check if this helped to solve our problem:

```
hannu=# select get_new_messages('52000');
                        get_new_messages
----------------------------------------------------------
 (200,"hello friend!",51993,"2012-01-09 02:23:28.470979")
 (200,"hello friend!",51994,"2012-01-09 02:23:28.470979")
 (200,"hello friend!",51996,"2012-01-09 02:23:28.470979")
 (200,"hello friend!",51997,"2012-01-09 02:23:28.470979")
 (200,"hello friend!",51998,"2012-01-09 02:23:28.470979")
 (200,"hello friend!",51999,"2012-01-09 02:23:28.470979")
 (200,"hello friend!",52000,"2012-01-09 02:23:28.470979")
(7 rows)
Time: 2.949 ms
```

Much better—indexed lookups are 300 times faster than sequential scans, and this difference will grow as tables get bigger!

As we are updating the messages and setting their status to read, it is also a good idea to set the fillfactor to something less than 100 percent.

> Fillfactor tells PostgreSQL not to fill up database pages completely but to leave some space for HOT updates. When PostgreSQL updates a row, it only marks the old row for deletion and adds a new row to the data file. If the row that is updated only changes unindexed fields and there is enough room in the page to store a second copy, a HOT update will be done instead. In this case, the copy can be found using original index pointers to the first copy, and no expensive index updates are done while updating.

```
hannu=# ALTER TABLE message SET (fillfactor = 90);
ALTER TABLE
Time: 75.729 ms
hannu=# CLUSTER message_from_user_ndx ON message;
CLUSTER
Time: 9797.639 ms

hannu=# select get_new_messages('55022');
                     get_new_messages
---------------------------------------------------------------
 (200,"hello friend!",55014,"2012-01-09 02:23:28.470979")
 (200,"hello friend!",55016,"2012-01-09 02:23:28.470979")
 (200,"hello friend!",55017,"2012-01-09 02:23:28.470979")
 (200,"hello friend!",55019,"2012-01-09 02:23:28.470979")
 (200,"hello friend!",55020,"2012-01-09 02:23:28.470979")
 (200,"hello friend!",55021,"2012-01-09 02:23:28.470979")
 (200,"hello friend!",55022,"2012-01-09 02:23:28.470979")
(7 rows)

Time: 1.895 ms
```

Still better. The fillfactor made the get_new_messages() function another 20 to 30 percent faster, thanks to enabling the faster HOT updates!

Dealing with success – splitting tables over multiple databases

Now, let's roll forward in time a little and assume you have been successful enough to attract tens of thousands of users and your single database starts creaking under the load.

My general rule of thumb is to start planning for a bigger machine or splitting the database when you are over 80 percent utilization at least for a few hours a day. It's good to have a plan earlier, but now you have to start doing something about really carrying out the plan.

What expansion plans work and when

There are a couple of popular ways to grow database-backed systems. Depending on your use case, not all ways will work.

Moving to a bigger server

If you suspect that you are near your top load for the service or product, you can simply move to a more powerful server. This may not be the best long-time scaling solution if you are still in the middle, or even in the beginning of your growth. You will run out of "bigger" machines to buy long before you are done. Servers also become disproportionately more expensive as the size increases, and you will be left with at least one "different" and thus not easily replaceable server once you implement a proper scaling solution.

On the other hand, this will work for some time and is often the easiest way to get some headroom while implementing real scaling solutions.

Master-slave replication – moving reads to slave

Master-slave replication, either trigger-based or WAL-based, works reasonably well in cases where the large majority of the database accesses are reads. Some things that fall under this case are website content managers, blogs, and other publishing systems.

As our chat system has more or less a 1:1 ratio of writes and reads, moving reads to a separate server will buy us nothing. The replication itself is more expensive than the possible win from reading from a second server.

Multimaster replication

Multi-master replication is even worse than master-slave(s) when the problem is scaling a write-heavy workload. It has all the problems of master-slave, plus it introduces extra load via cross-partition locking or conflict resolution requirements, which further slows down the whole cluster.

Data partitioning across multiple servers

The obvious solution to scaling writes is to split them between several servers. Ideally you could have, for example, four servers and each of them getting exactly ¼th of the load.

In this case, each server would hold a quarter of users and messages, and serve a quarter of all requests.

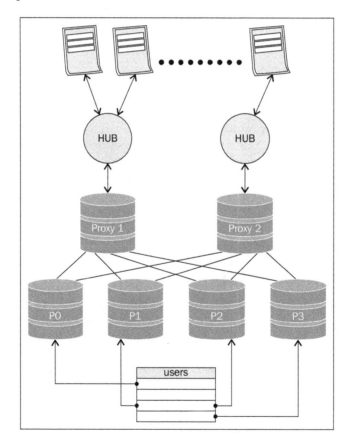

To make the change transparent for database clients, we introduce a layer of proxy databases. These proxy databases can either reside on the same hosts as the partition databases or be on their own host. The role of the proxy databases is to pretend to be the database for clients, but in fact delegate the real work to partitions by calling the right function in the right partition database.

This client transparency is not terribly important if you have just one application accessing the database. If you did, you could then do the splitting in the client application. It becomes very handy as your system grows to have several applications, perhaps using many different platforms and frameworks on the client side.

Having a separate layer of proxy databases enables easy management of data splitting so that the client applications don't need to know anything about the underlying data architecture. They just call the functions they need and that's all they need to know. In fact, you can switch out the whole database structure without the clients ever noticing anything except the better performance from the new architecture.

More on how exactly the proxy works later. For now, let us tackle splitting the data.

Splitting the data

If we split the data, we need a simple and efficient way to determine which server stores each data row. If the data had an integer primary key, you could just go round-robin, store the first row on the first server, the second row on the second, and so on. This would give you a fairly even distribution, even when rows with certain IDs are missing.

The partitioning function for selecting between four servers would be simply:

```
partition_nr = id & 3
```

The partitioning mask 3 (binary 11) is for the first two bits. For eight partitions, you would use 7 (binary 111), and for 64 servers it would be 63 (00111111). It is not as easy with things like usernames, where putting all names starting with an A first, B second, and so on does not produce an even distribution.

Turning the username into a fairly evenly distributed integer via the hash function solves this problem and can be used directly to select the partition.

```
partition_nr = hashtext(username) & 3
```

This would distribute the users in the following manner:

```
hannu=# SELECT username, hashtext(username) & 3 as partition_nr FROM
user_info;
-[ RECORD 1 ]+--------
username     | bob
partition_nr | 1
-[ RECORD 2 ]+--------
username     | jane
partition_nr | 2
-[ RECORD 3 ]+--------
username     | tom
partition_nr | 1
-[ RECORD 4 ]+--------
username     | mary
partition_nr | 3
-[ RECORD 5 ]+--------
username     | jill
partition_nr | 2
-[ RECORD 6 ]+--------
username     | abigail
partition_nr | 3
-[ RECORD 7 ]+--------
username     | ted
partition_nr | 3
-[ RECORD 8 ]+--------
username     | alfonso
partition_nr | 0
```

So partition 0 gets user `alfonso`, partition 1 `bob` and `tom`, partition 2 `jane` and `jill`, and partition 3 gets `mary`, `abigail`, and `ted`. The distribution is not exactly ¼th to each partition; but as the number of partitions increase, it will be pretty close where this actually matters.

If we had no PL/Proxy language, we could write the partitioning functions in the most untrusted PL languages. For example, a simple login proxy function written in PL/Pythonu looks like this:

```
CREATE OR REPLACE FUNCTION login(
    IN i_username text, IN i_pwdhash text,
    OUT status int, OUT message text )
AS $$
    import psycopg2
    partitions = [
        'dbname=chap9p0 port=5433',
```

```
        'dbname=chap9p1 port=5433',
        'dbname=chap9p2 port=5433',
        'dbname=chap9p3 port=5433',
    ]
    partition_nr = hash(i_username) & 3
    con = psycopg2.connect(partitions[partition_nr])
    cur = con.cursor()
    cur.execute('select * from login(%s,%s)', ( i_username, i_
pwdhash))
    status, message = cur.fetchone()
    return (status, message)
$$ LANGUAGE plpythonu SECURITY DEFINER;
```

Here, we defined a set of four partition databases, given by their connect strings stored as a list in variable partitions.

When executing the function, we first evaluate the hash function on the username argument (hash(i_username)) and extract two bits from it (& 3) to get index into the partitions list (the partition number) for executing each call.

Then, we open a connection to a partition database using the connect string selected by the partition number (con=psycopg2.connect(partitions[partition_nr])).

Finally, we execute a remote query in the partition database and return the results of this to the caller of this proxy function.

This works reasonably well if implemented like this, but also has at least two places where it is suboptimal:

- First, it opens a new database connection each time the function is called, which kills performance
- Second, it is a maintenance nightmare if you hard-wire the partition information in full in all functions

The performance problem can be solved by caching the open connections, and the maintenance problem can be solved by having a single function returning the partition information. However, even when we do these changes and stay with PL/Pythonu for partitioning, we will still be doing a lot of copy and paste programming in each of our proxy functions.

Once we had reached the preceding conclusions when growing our database systems at Skype, the next logical step was quite obvious. We needed a special partitioning language, which would do just this one thing—calling remote SQL functions, and then make it as fast as possible; and thus the PL/Proxy database partitioning language was born.

PL/Proxy – the partitioning language

The rest of this chapter is devoted to the PL/Proxy language. First, we will install it. Then, we will look at its syntax and ways to configure the partitions for its use. Finally, we will discuss how to do the actual data migration from a single database to a partitioned one and then look at several usage examples.

Installing PL/Proxy

If you are on Debian, Ubuntu, or a Red Hat variant, installing the language is easy.

1. First, you have to install the required packages on your operating system:

    ```
    sudo apt-get install postgresql-9.2-plproxy
    ```

    Or:

    ```
    sudo yum install plproxy92
    ```

2. Then, install the language in the database as an extension, which will be hosting the PL/Proxy functions:

    ```
    -bash-4.2$ psql -c "CREATE EXTENSION plproxy" proxy1
    CREATE EXTENSION
    ```

> At the time of writing this book, the PL/Proxy language is still not completely integrated with the PostgreSQL standard distribution. The SQL commands CREATE LANGUAGE plproxy and its command-line equivalent createlang plproxy do not work. This may have been fixed by the time you read this, so you can try these first.

PL/Proxy language syntax

The PL/Proxy language itself is very simple. The purpose of a PL/Proxy function is to hand off the processing to another server so that it only needs six statements:

*   CONNECT or CLUSTER and RUN ON for selecting the target database partition
*   SELECT and TARGET for specifying the query to run
*   SPLIT for splitting an ARRAY argument between several sub-arrays for running on multiple partitions

CONNECT, CLUSTER, and RUN ON

The first group of statements handle the remote connectivity to the partitions. The help determines which database to run the query on. You specify the exact partition to run the query using CONNECT:

```
CONNECT 'connect string' ;
```

Here, connect string determines the database to run. connect string is the standard PostgreSQL connect string you would use to connect to the database from a client application, for example: dbname=p0 port=5433.

Or, you can specify a name using CLUSTER:

```
CLUSTER 'usercluster'; -
```

Or finally, you can specify a partition number using RUN ON:

```
RUN ON part_func(arg[, ...]) ;
```

part_func() can be any existing or user-defined PostgreSQL function returning an integer. PL/Proxy calls that function with the given arguments and then uses N lower bits from the result to select a connection to a cluster partition.

There are two more versions of the RUN ON statement:

```
RUN ON ANY;
```

This means that the function can be executed on any partition in a cluster. This can be used when all the required data for a function is present on all partitions.

The other version is:

```
RUN ON ALL;
```

This runs the statement on all partitions in parallel and then returns a concatenation of results from the partitions. This has at least three main uses:

- For cases when you don't know where the required data row is, like when getting data using non-partition keys. For example, getting a user by its e-mail when the table is partitioned by username.

- Running aggregate functions over larger subsets of data, say counting all users. For example, getting all the users who have a certain user in their friend's lists.

- Manipulating data that needs to be the same on all partitions. For example, when you have a price list that other functions are using, then one simple way to manage this price list is using a RUN ON ALL function.

SELECT and TARGET

The default behavior of a PL/Proxy function if no SELECT or TARGET is present is to call the function with the exact same signature as itself in the remote partition.

Suppose we have the function:

```
CREATE OR REPLACE FUNCTION login(
    IN i_username text, IN i_pwdhash text,
    OUT status int, OUT message text )
AS $$
    CONNECT 'dbname=chap9 host=10.10.10.1';
$$ LANGUAGE plproxy SECURITY DEFINER;
```

If it is defined in schema public, the following call select * from login('bob', 'secret') connects to the database chap9 on host 10.10.10.1 and runs the following SQL statement there:

```
SELECT * FROM public.login('bob', 'secret')
```

This retrieves the result and returns it to its caller.

If you don't want to define a function inside the remote database, you can substitute the default select * from <thisfunction>(<arg1>, ...) call with your own by writing it in the function body of PL/Proxy function:

```
CREATE OR REPLACE FUNCTION get_user_email(i_username text)
RETURNS SETOF text AS $$
    CONNECT 'dbname=chap9 host=10.10.10.1';
    SELECT email FROM user_info where username =  i_username;
$$ LANGUAGE plproxy SECURITY DEFINER;
```

Only a single SELECT is supported; for any other or more complex SQL statements, you have to write a remote function and call it.

The third option is to still call a function similar to itself, but named differently. For example, if you have a proxy function defined not in a separate proxy database, but in a partition, you may want it to target the local database for some data:

```
CREATE OR REPLACE FUNCTION public.get_user_email(i_username text)
RETURNS SETOF text AS $$
    CLUSTER 'messaging';
    RUN ON hashtext(i_username);
    TARGET local.get_user_email;
$$ LANGUAGE plproxy SECURITY DEFINER;
```

In this setup, the local version of get_user_email() is in schema local on all partitions. Therefore, if one of the partitions connects back to the same database that it is defined in, it avoids circular calling.

SPLIT – distributing array elements over several partitions

The last PL/Proxy statement is for cases where you want some bigger chunk of work to be done in appropriate partitions. For example, if you have a function to create several users in one call and you still want to be able to use it after partitioning, the SPLIT statement is a way to tell PL/Proxy to split the arrays between the partitions based on the partitioning function:

```
CREATE or REPLACE FUNCTION create_new_users(
    IN i_username text[], IN i_pwdhash text[], IN i_email text[],
    OUT status int, OUT message text )  RETURNS SETOF RECORD
AS $$
BEGIN
  FOR i IN 1..array_length(i_username,1) LOOP
     SELECT *
       INTO status, message
       FROM new_user(i_username[i], i_pwdhash[i], i_email[i]);
     RETURN NEXT;
  END LOOP;
END;
$$ LANGUAGE plpgsql SECURITY DEFINER;
```

The following PL/Proxy function definition created on the proxy database can be used to split the calls across the partitions:

```
CREATE or REPLACE FUNCTION create_new_users(
    IN i_username text[], IN i_pwdhash text[], IN i_email text[],
    OUT status int, OUT message text )  RETURNS SETOF RECORD
AS $$
  CLUSTER 'messaging';
  RUN ON hashtext(i_username);
  SPLIT  i_username,  i_pwdhash,  i_email;
$$ LANGUAGE plproxy SECURITY DEFINER;
```

It would be called by sending in three arrays to the function:

```
SELECT * FROM create_new_users(
    ARRAY['bob', 'jane', 'tom'],
    ARRAY[md5('bobs_pwd'), md5('janes_pwd'), md5('toms_pwd')],
    ARRAY['bob@mail.com', 'jane@mail.com', 'tom@mail.com']
);
```

It will result in two parallel calls to partitions 1 and 2 (as using `hashtext(i_username)` tom and bob map to partition 1 and mary to partition 2 of total for partitions as explained earlier), with the following arguments for partition 1:

```
SELECT * FROM create_new_users(
    ARRAY['bob', 'tom'],
    ARRAY['6c6e5b564fb0b192f66b2a0a60c751bb',
              'edcc36c33f7529f430a1bc6eb7191dfe'],
    ARRAY['bob@mail.com','tom@mail.com']
);
```

And this for partition 2:

```
SELECT * FROM create_new_users(
    ARRAY['jane'],
    ARRAY['cbbf391d3ef4c60afd851d851bda2dc8'],
    ARRAY['jane@mail.com']
);
```

Then, it returns a concatenation of the results:

```
status | message
-------+---------
   200 | OK
   200 | OK
   200 | OK
(3 rows)
```

Distribution of data

First, what is a cluster in PL/Proxy? Well, the cluster is a set of partitions that make up the whole database. Each cluster consists of a number of partitions as determined by the cluster configuration. Each partition is uniquely specified by its connect string. The list of connection strings is what makes up a cluster. The position of the partition in this list is what determines the partition number, so the first element in the list is partition 0, the second partition is 1, and so on.

The partition is selected by the output of the RUN ON function, and then masked by the right number of bits to map it on partitions. So, if `hashtext(i_username)` returns 14 and there are four partitions (2 bits, mask binary 11 or 3 in decimal), the partition number will be 14 and 3 = 2, and the function will be called on partition 2 (starting from zero), which is the third element in partition list.

The constraint that the number of partitions has to be a power of two may seem an unnecessary restriction at first, but it was done in order to make sure that it is, and it will remain to be, easy to expand the number of partitions without the need to redistribute all the data.

For example, if you tried to move from three partitions to four, most likely 3/4th of the data rows in partitions 0 to 2 have to be moved to new partitions to evenly cover 0 to 3. On the other hand, when moving from four to eight partitions, the data for partitions 0 and 1 is exactly the same that was previously on partition 0, 2-3 is old 1 and so on. That is, your data does not need to be moved immediately, and half of the data does not need to be moved at all.

The actual configuration of the cluster, the definition of partitions can be done in two ways, either by using a set of functions in schema plproxy, or you can take advantage of the SQL/MED connection management. (SQL/MED is available starting PostgreSQL 8.4 and above.)

Configuring PL/Proxy cluster using functions

This is the original way to configure PL/Proxy, which works on all versions of PostgreSQL. When a query needs to be forwarded to a remote database, the function plproxy.get_cluster_partitions(cluster) is invoked by PL/Proxy to get the connection string to use for each partition.

The following function is an example which returns information for a cluster with four partitions, p0 to p3:

```
CREATE OR REPLACE FUNCTION plproxy.get_cluster_partitions(cluster_name
text)
RETURNS SETOF text AS $$
BEGIN
    IF cluster_name = 'messaging' THEN
        RETURN NEXT 'dbname=p0';
        RETURN NEXT 'dbname=p1';
        RETURN NEXT 'dbname=p2';
        RETURN NEXT 'dbname=p3';
    ELSE
        RAISE EXCEPTION 'Unknown cluster';
    END IF;
END;
$$ LANGUAGE plpgsql;
```

A production application might query some configuration tables or even read some configuration files to return the connection strings. Once again, the number of partitions returned must be a power of two. If you are absolutely sure that some partitions are never used, you can return empty strings for these.

We also need to define a `plproxy.get_cluster_version(cluster_name)` function. This is called on each request and if the cluster version has not changed, the output from a cached result from `plproxy.get_cluster_partitions` can be reused. So, it is best to make sure that this function is as fast as possible:

```
CREATE OR REPLACE FUNCTION plproxy.get_cluster_version(cluster_name
text)
RETURNS int4 AS $$
BEGIN
    IF cluster_name = 'messaging' THEN
        RETURN 1;
    ELSE
        RAISE EXCEPTION 'Unknown cluster';
    END IF;
END;
$$ LANGUAGE plpgsql;
```

The last function needed is `plproxy.get_cluster_config`, which enables you to configure the behavior of PL/Proxy. This sample will set the connection lifetime to 10 minutes:

```
CREATE OR REPLACE FUNCTION plproxy.get_cluster_config(
    in cluster_name text,
    out key text,
    out val text)
RETURNS SETOF record AS $$
BEGIN
    -- lets use same config for all clusters
    key := 'connection_lifetime';
    val := 10*60;
    RETURN NEXT;
    RETURN;
END;
$$ LANGUAGE plpgsql;
```

Configuring PL/Proxy cluster using SQL/MED

Since version 8.4, PostgreSQL has support for an SQL standard for management of external data, usually referred to as SQL/MED. SQL/MED is simply a standard way to access data that resides outside the database. Using functions to configure partitions is arguably insecure, as any caller of `plproxy.get_cluster_partitions()` can learn connection strings for partitions that may contain sensitive info like passwords. PL/Proxy also provides a way to do the cluster configuration using SQL/MED, which follows the standard SQL security practices.

The same configuration as discussed earlier, when done using SQL/MED is as follows:

1. First, create a foreign data wrapper called `plproxy`:

    ```
    proxy1=# CREATE FOREIGN DATA WRAPPER plproxy;
    ```

2. Then create an external server that defines both the connection options and the partitions:

    ```
    proxy1=# CREATE SERVER messaging FOREIGN DATA WRAPPER plproxy
    proxy1-# OPTIONS (connection_lifetime '1800',
    proxy1(#           p0 'dbname=p0',
    proxy1(#           p1 'dbname=p1',
    proxy1(#           p2 'dbname=p2',
    proxy1(#           p3 'dbname=p3'
    proxy1(# )
    CREATE SERVER
    ```

3. Finally, grant usage on this server to either `PUBLIC` so all users can use it:

    ```
    proxy1=# CREATE USER MAPPING FOR PUBLIC SERVER messaging;
    CREATE USER MAPPING
    ```

    Or, to some specific users or groups:

    ```
    proxy1=# CREATE USER MAPPING FOR bob SERVER  messaging
    proxy1-#  OPTIONS (user 'plproxy', password 'very.secret');
    CREATE USER MAPPING
    ```

4. Then, grant usage on the cluster to the users who need to use it:

    ```
    proxy1=# GRANT USAGE ON FOREIGN SERVER messaging TO bob;
    GRANT
    ```

 More info on SQL/MED as implemented in PostgreSQL can be found at `http://www.postgresql.org/docs/current/static/sql-createforeigndatawrapper.html`.

Moving data from the single to the partitioned database

If you can schedule some downtime and your new partition databases are as big as your original single database, the easiest way to partition the data is to make a full copy of each of the nodes and then simply delete the rows that do not belong to the partition:

```
pg_dump chap9 | psql p0
psql p0 -c 'delete from message where hashtext(to_user) & 3 <> 0'
psql p0 -c 'delete from user_info where hashtext(username) & 3 <> 0'
```

Repeat this for partitions p1 to p3, each time deleting rows which don't match the partition number (`psql chap9p1 -c 'delete … & 3 <> 1`).

 Remember to vacuum when you are finished deleting the rows. PostgreSQL will leave the dead rows in the data tables, so do a little maintenance while you have some downtime.

When trying to delete from `user_info`, you will notice that you can't do it without dropping a foreign key from `messages.from_user`.

Here, we could decide that it is OK to keep the messages on the receivers partition only, and if needed, that the sent messages can be retrieved using a RUN ON ALL function. So, we will drop the foreign key from `messages.from_user`.

```
psql p0 -c 'alter table message drop constraint message_from_user_fkey
```

There are other options when splitting the data that requires less disk space usage for database system if you are willing to do more manual work.

For example, you can copy over just the schema using `pg_dump -s` and then use `COPY` from an SQL statement to move over just the needed rows:

```
pg_dump -s chap9 | psql p0
psql chap9 -c "COPY (select * from messages where hashtext(to_user) & 3 =
0) TO stdout" | psql p0 -c 'COPY messages FROM stdin'
...
```

Or even set up a specially designed Londiste replica and do the switch from single database to partitioned cluster in only seconds once the replica has reached a stable state.

Summary

In this chapter, we have gone over the process of database sharding for databases that are too big to take the write load on a single host, or where you just want to have the added resilience of having a system, where one host being down does not bring the whole system down.

In short, the process is:

- Decide which tables you want to split over multiple hosts
- Add the partition databases and move the data
- Set up the proxy functions for all the functions accessing those tables
- Watch for a little while that everything is working
- Relax

Also, we also took a brief look at using PL/Proxy for simple remote queries to other PostgreSQL databases, which may be handy for some tasks even after the new **Foreign Data Wrapper (FDW)** functionality in PostgreSQL replaced it for many uses.

While PL/Proxy is not for everyone, it may well save the day if you are suddenly faced with rapid database growth and have the need for an easy and clean way to spread the database over many hosts.

10
Publishing Your Code as PostgreSQL Extensions

If you are new to PostgreSQL, now is the time to dance for joy.

Now that you're done dancing, I'll tell you why. You have managed to avoid the "bad old days" of contrib modules. Contrib modules are the installation systems that were used to install related PostgreSQL objects prior to Version 9.1. They may be additional data types, enhanced management functions, or just really any type of module you want to add to PostgreSQL. They consist of any group of related functions, views, tables, operators, types, and indexes that were lumped into an installation file and committed to the database in one fell swoop. Unfortunately, contrib modules only provided for installation, and nothing else. In fact, they were not really an installation system at all. They were just some unrelated SQL scripts that happened to install everything that the author thought you needed.

PostgreSQL extensions provide many new services that a package management system should have. Well...at least the ones that module authors complained the most about not being present.

Some of the new features that you will be introduced to in this chapter include versioning, dependencies, updates, and removal.

When to create an extension

Well, first you have to understand that extensions are all about togetherness. Once the objects from a contrib module were installed, PostgreSQL provided no way to show a relationship between them. This led many developers to create their own (and sometimes rather ingenious) methods to version, update, upgrade, and uninstall all of the necessary "stuff" to get a feature to work.

So, the first question to ask yourself when contemplating a PostgreSQL extension as a way to publish your code is, "How does all of the "stuff" in my extension relate together?"

This question will help you make extensions that are as granular as reasonable. If the objective is to enhance PostgreSQL with the ability to provide an inventory management system, maybe it would be better to start with an extension that provides a bill of material's data type first, and subsequently build additional extensions that are dependent upon that one. The moral of the story is to dream big, but create each extension with only the smallest number of related items that make sense.

A good example of an extension that provides a feature to PostgreSQL is OpenFTS. This extension provides full text searching capabilities to PostgreSQL by creating data types, indexes, and functions that are well related to each other.

Another type of extension is PostGIS, which provides a rich set of tools to deal with geographic information systems. Although this extension provides many more bits of functionality than OpenFTS, it is still as granular as possible by virtue of the fact that everything that is provided is necessary for geographic software development.

Possibly you are a book author, and the only relationship that the objects in your extension have is that they need to be conveniently removed when your poor victim ...ahem...the reader is through with them. Welcome to the wonders of extensions.

For a list of very useful extensions that have gained some community popularity, you might want to take a look at this page fairly often:

`http://www.postgresql.org/download/products/6/`

You should also take a look at the PostgreSQL extension network at `http://www.pgxn.org`.

To find out what objects can be packaged into an extension, look at the ALTER EXTENSION ADD command in the PostgreSQL documentation:

`http://www.postgresql.org/docs/current/static/sql-alterextension.html`

Unpackaged extensions

Starting with Version 9.1, PostgreSQL provides a convenient way to move from the primordial ooze of unversioned contrib modules into the brave new world of extensions. Basically, you provide an SQL file to show the relationship of the objects to the extension. The contrib module's cube provides a good example of this in cube--unpackaged--1.0.sql:

```
/* contrib/cube/cube--unpackaged--1.0.sql */

-- complain if script is sourced in psql, rather than via CREATE
EXTENSION
\echo Use "CREATE EXTENSION cube" to load this file. \quit

ALTER EXTENSION cube ADD type cube,
ALTER EXTENSION cube ADD function cube_in(cstring);
ALTER EXTENSION cube ADD function cube(double precision[],double
precision[]);
ALTER EXTENSION cube ADD function cube(double precision[]);
...
```

The code that provides multidimensional cubes for PostgreSQL has been stable for quite some time. It is unlikely that a new version will be created any time soon. The only reason for this module to be converted into an extension is to allow for easy installation and removal.

You would then execute the command:

```
CREATE EXTENSION cube FROM unpackaged;
```

The unrelated items are now grouped together into the extension named cube. This also makes it easier for the packaging maintainer on any platform to include your extension into the repository. We'll show you how to make the packages to install your extension in the *Building an extension* section.

Extension versions

The version mechanism for PostgreSQL extensions is simple. Name it whatever you want and give it whatever alphanumeric version number that suits your fancy. Easy, eh? Just name the files with this format:

extension--version.sql

If you want to provide an upgrade path from one version of your extension to another, you would provide the file:

extension--oldversion--newversion.sql

This simple mechanism allows PostgreSQL to update an extension that is already in place. Gone are the days of painful exporting and re-importing data just to change the definition of a data type. So, let's go ahead and update our example extension using the file `postal--1.0--1.1.sql`. This update is as easy as:

```
ALTER EXTENSION postal UPDATE TO '1.1';
```

A note of caution: PostgreSQL does not have any concept of what your version number means. In this example, the extension was updated from Version 1.0 to 1.1 because we explicitly provided a script for that specific conversion. PostgreSQL did not deduce that 1.1 follows 1.0. We could have just as easily used the names of fruits or historical battleships for our version numbers and the result would have been the same.

PostgreSQL will use multiple update files if necessary to achieve the desired result. Given the following command:

```
ALTER EXTENSION postal UPDATE TO '1.4';
```

PostgreSQL will apply the files `postal--1.1--1.2.sql`, `postal--1.2--1.3.sql` and `postal--1.3--1.4.sql` in the correct order to achieve the desired version.

You may also use this technique to provide upgrade scripts that are in fact downgrade scripts, that is, they actually remove functionality. Be careful with this, though. If a path to a desired version is to downgrade before an upgrade, PostgreSQL will take the shortest route. This may result in some unintended results, including data loss. My advice would be to not provide downgrade scripts. The risk just isn't worth it.

The .control file

Along with the extension installation script file, you must provide a `.control` file. The `.control` file for our example `postal.control` looks like this:

```
# postal address processing extension
comment = 'utilities for postal processing'
default_version = '1.0'
module_pathname = '$libdir/postal'
relocatable = truerequires = plpgsql
```

The purpose of the `.control` file is to provide a description of your extension. This metadata may include `directory`, `default_version`, `comment`, `encoding`, `module_pathname`, `requires`, `superuser`, `relocatable`, and `schema`.

The main PostgreSQL documentation for this file is located at `http://www.postgresql.org/docs/current/static/extend-extensions.html`.

This example shows a `requires` configuration parameter. Our extension depends on the procedural language PL/pgSQL. On most platforms, it is installed by default. Unfortunately, it is not installed on all platforms, and nothing should be taken for granted.

Multiple dependencies can be indicated by separating them with commas. This is very handy when constructing a set of services based on multiple extensions.

As we mentioned in the previous section, PostgreSQL does not provide any interpretation of the version number of an extension. Versions can be names as well as numbers, so there is no way for PostgreSQL to interpret that `postal--lamb.sql` comes before `postal--sheep.sql`. This design limitation poses a problem to the extension developer, in that there is no way to specify that your extension depends on a specific version of another extension. I would love to see this configuration parameter enhanced with a syntax like `requires = postgis >= 1.3`, but alas, no such construction exists at the moment.

Building an extension

We have already covered the basics of creating a script file and a `.control` file. Actually, that is all that is necessary for a PostgreSQL extension. You may simply copy these files into the shared extension directory on your computer and execute the following command:

```
CREATE EXTENSION postal;
```

This will install your extension into the currently selected database.

The shared extension path is dependent on how PostgreSQL is installed, but for Ubuntu, it is `/usr/share/postgresql/9.2/extension`.

However, there is a much better way to do this that works with any package manager on any platform.

PostgreSQL provides an extension building toolkit as a part of the server development package. To install this package on Ubuntu, you can type:

```
sudo apt-get install postgresql-dev-9.2
```

This will install all of the PostgreSQL source code necessary to create and install an extension. You would then create a file named `Makefile` in the same directory as the rest of your extension files. The content of this file looks like this:

```
EXTENSION = postal

DATA = postal--1.0.sql


PG_CONFIG = pg_config

PGXS := $(shell $(PG_CONFIG) --pgxs)

include $(PGXS)
```

This simple `Makefile` file will copy your extension script file and the `.control` file into the proper shared extension directory on any platform. Invoke it with this command:

sudo make install

You will see some output like this:

```
/bin/mkdir -p '/usr/share/postgresql/9.1/extension'
```

```
/bin/sh /usr/lib/postgresql/9.1/lib/pgxs/src/makefiles/../../config/
install-sh -c -m 644 ./postal.control '/usr/share/postgresql/9.1/
extension/'
```

```
/bin/sh /usr/lib/postgresql/9.1/lib/pgxs/src/makefiles/../../config/
install-sh -c -m 644 ./postal--1.0.sql  '/usr/share/postgresql/9.1/
extension/'
```

Your extension is now located in the proper directory for installation. You can install it into the current database with:

CREATE EXTENSION postal;

You will then see the confirmation text letting you know that you have now gone postal:

CREATE EXTENSION

Installing an extension

Extensions that have been packaged for you by your friendly distribution manager are very simple to install using the following command:

```
CREATE EXTENSION extension_name;
```

Most of the popular Linux distributions include a package called something like `postgresql-contrib-9.2`. This naming convention is left over from the contrib style installation of PostgreSQL objects. Don't worry, for PostgreSQL 9.2 this package will actually provide extensions rather than contrib modules.

To find out where the files were placed on Ubuntu 10.04 Linux, you can execute the following command:

```
pg_config --sharedir
```

This will show you the shared component's installation directory:

```
/usr/share/postgresql/9.2
```

The extensions will be located in a directory called extension, immediately below the shared directory. This will then be named `/usr/share/postgresql/9.2/extension`.

To see what extensions are available for you to install, try this command:

```
ls $(pg_config -sharedir)/extension/*.control
```

This will show you all the extensions that have been made available to you by your Linux distribution package management system.

For extensions that you have created yourself, you must copy your SQL script file and the `.control` file to the shared extension directory before invoking CREATE EXTENSION in PostgreSQL.

```
cp postal.control postal--1.0.sql $(pg_config --sharedir)/extension
```

To see the procedure for doing this reliably on any target platform, refer to the *Building an Extension* section.

Publishing your extension

Thank you for contributing to the PostgreSQL community! Your support will not go unnoticed in this gathering of like-minded guys that are all a slightly smarter than each other. Your work will be seen by dozens of developers looking for community solutions to common problems. You have made the open source world a better place.

Since we are talking about publication, you should consider the licensing model for your extension. The publication methods that we are about to describe assume that the extension will be made available to the general public. As such, please consider the PostgreSQL license for your extension. You can find the current one here:

```
http://www.postgresql.org/about/licence/
```

Introduction to the PostgreSQL Extension Network

When you want to publish your module, you could start writing packaging scripts for each of the distribution systems for every operating system. This is the way the PostgreSQL extensions have been distributed in the past. This distribution system has not been very friendly to the open source community, or very well received. In an effort to make extension publication more palatable, a group of open source writers and backing companies got together and founded the PostgreSQL Extension Network.

The PostgreSQL Extension Network `http://pgxn.org/` provides a central repository for your open source extensions. By the kindness of the maintainers, it also provides installation scripts for your extensions that will work on most of the popular PostgreSQL deployment operating systems.

Signing up to publish your extension

To sign up to publish your extension, perform the following steps:

1. Start by requesting an account on the management page:
   `http://manager.pgxn.org`.

2. Click on **Request Account** and fill in your personal information. The PostgreSQL Extension Network folks will get back to you via e-mail after an actual human processes your sign up request.

3. Click on the provided link in the e-mail to confirm your account and set a new password on the PGXN website:

> **Subject:** Welcome to PGXN!
> **From:** "PGXN Admins" <pgxn@pgexperts.com>
> **Date:** Tue, March 6, 2012 10:20 am
> **To:** "bithead" <kirk@webfinish.com>
> **Priority:** Normal
> **Options:** View Full Header | View Printable Version | Download this as a file
>
> ---
>
> What up, bithead.
>
> Your PGXN account request has been approved. Ready to get started?
> Great! Just click this link to set your password and get going:
>
>   https://manager.pgxn.org/account/reset/nvrmG
>
> Best,
>
> PGXN Management

This site does not have a secure certificate that any of the common Internet browsers support. The first thing you will see is a page to confirm that you have not made an error in coming here:

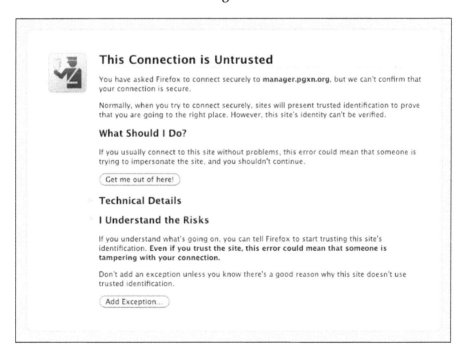

This Connection is Untrusted

You have asked Firefox to connect securely to **manager.pgxn.org**, but we can't confirm that your connection is secure.

Normally, when you try to connect securely, sites will present trusted identification to prove that you are going to the right place. However, this site's identity can't be verified.

What Should I Do?

If you usually connect to this site without problems, this error could mean that someone is trying to impersonate the site, and you shouldn't continue.

(Get me out of here!)

Technical Details

I Understand the Risks

If you understand what's going on, you can tell Firefox to start trusting this site's identification. **Even if you trust the site, this error could mean that someone is tampering with your connection.**

Don't add an exception unless you know there's a good reason why this site doesn't use trusted identification.

(Add Exception...)

4. Confirm the server certificate by adding an exception to the browser rules. Click on **Add Exception** and in the next screen make the exception permanent:

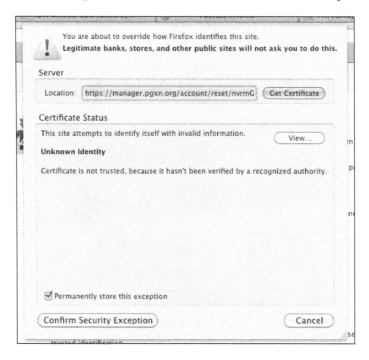

5. Click on **Confirm Security Exception**.

You will then be prompted to create a password for your account:

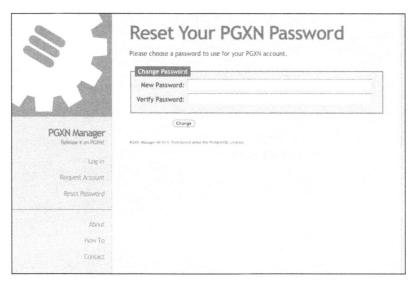

6. Set a password that you will remember, and confirm by typing it again. Click on **Change** and you will be welcomed to the site:

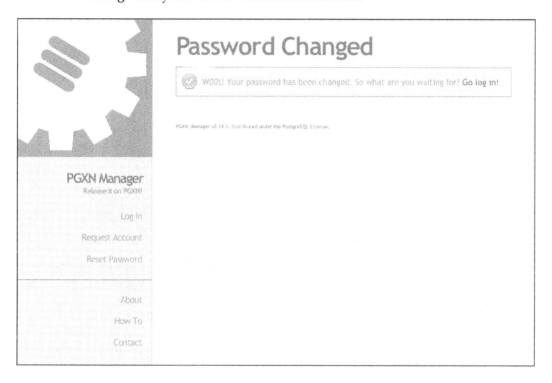

That is all there is to getting signed up. Once you have your new account set up, you can do some things that will make PostgreSQL extension programming much more painless.

Creating an extension project the easy way

First, let's install some utility packages that will create a lot of boilerplate files that we have already described in earlier sections:

```
apt-get install ruby
apt-get install rubygems
apt-get install ruby1.8-dev
apt-get install libopenssl-ruby1.8
gem install rubygems-update
/var/lib/gems/1.8/bin/update_rubygems
gem install pgxn_utils
```

You will now find that you have a utility installed named `pgxn-utils`. This utility makes it super simple to create an extension project.

```
pgxn-utils skeleton myextension
      create   myextension
      create   myextension/myextension.control
      create   myextension/META.json
      create   myextension/Makefile
      create   myextension/README.md
      create   myextension/doc/myextension.md
      create   myextension/sql/myextension.sql
      create   myextension/sql/uninstall_myextension.sql
      create   myextension/test/expected/base.out
      create   myextension/test/sql/base.sql
```

Wow! All of the files that we have mentioned so far just got created in a single step. Several files also got created to support the old contrib style of deployment. The next few sections will show which ones are important to you for extension development.

This package management system has one notable restriction. In contrast to PostgreSQL, which allows version numbers to be any alphanumeric text, this package management requires version numbers to follow the rules of semantic versioning. This version format includes major version, minor version, and release number in the format `major.minor.release`. This is to assist the package manager in installing your package on multiple operating system platforms. Just go with it, you'll thank us later.

Providing the metadata about the extension

There are three files used to provide data about the extension. The PostgreSQL Extension Network uses one of them on the website, `META.json`, for search criteria and description text for the extension. `META.json` will be located in `myextension/META.json`.

Here is an example:

```
{
    "name": "myextension",
    "abstract": "A short description",
    "description": "A long description",
    "version": "0.0.1",
    "maintainer": "The maintainer's name",
```

```
    "license": "postgresql",
    "provides": {
        "myextension": {
            "abstract": "A short description",
            "file": "sql/myextension.sql",
            "docfile": "doc/myextension.md",
            "version": "0.0.1"
        }
    },
    "release_status": "unstable",

    "generated_by": "The maintainer's name",


    "meta-spec": {
        "version": "1.0.0",
        "url": "http://pgxn.org/meta/spec.txt"
    }
}
```

You should add some sections to it to describe your keywords and any additional resources that you make available to the user. These sections would look like this:

```
"tags": [
  "cures cancer",
  "myextension",
  "creates world peace"
],
"resources": {
  "bugtracker":
      {"web": "https://github.com/myaccount/myextension/issues/"},
  "repository": {
      "type": "git",
      "url": "git://github.com/myaccount/myextension.git",
      "web": "https://github.com/myaccount/myextension/"
    }
  }
```

The complete file would then look like this:

```
{
    "name": "myextension",
    "abstract": "A short description",
    "description": "A long description",
    "version": "0.0.1",
```

```
    "maintainer": "The maintainer's name",
    "license": "postgresql",
    "provides": {
        "myextension": {
            "abstract": "A short description",
            "file": "sql/myextension.sql",
            "docfile": "doc/myextension.md",
            "version": "0.0.1"
        }
    },
    "release_status": "unstable",

    "generated_by": "The maintainer's name",


    "meta-spec": {
        "version": "1.0.0",
        "url": "http://pgxn.org/meta/spec.txt"
    }
     "tags": [
        "cures cancer",
        "myextension",
        "creates world peace"
    ],
        "resources": {
        "bugtracker":
        {"web": "https://github.com/myaccount/myextension/issues/"},
        "repository": {
        "type": "git",
        "url": "git://github.com/myaccount/myextension.git",
        "web": "https://github.com/myaccount/myextension/"
        }
     }
    }
```

The next file that you will need to modify is README.md. This file is located in
myextension/README.md. An example is provided with the code that accompanies
this book. Due to the length, it will not be reproduced here. This file is distributed
along with your extension. It is a plain text file that is meant for human consumption.
Describe anything you like in it. Mine includes a recipe for doner kebabs. Quite
tasty! But most importantly, put a nice long description of the benefits and ease of
use of your extension. Finally, we come to doc/myextension.md. This file is used
by the PostgreSQL Extension Network to provide a very nice landing page for your
extension. It will look something like this:

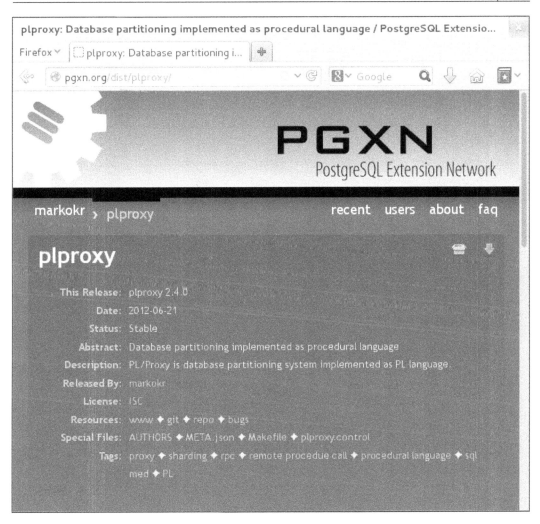

This file is formatted with wiki text markup. You may use several different markup syntaxes here. A discussion of wiki markup is beyond the scope of this description, but the formatting that is in the example is likely to be all that you will ever need anyway.

Here is an example of the content of the file:

```
myextension
===========

Synopsis
--------
```

```
      Show a brief synopsis of the extension.

   Description
   -----------

   A long description

   Usage
   -----

      Show usage.

   Support
   -------

      There is issues tracker? Github? Put this information here.

   Author
   ------

   [The maintainer's name]

   Copyright and License
   ---------------------

   Copyright (c) 2012 The maintainer's name.
```

Fill out the file with some descriptive narrative about your extension. Add anything that you think might be relevant to the developer that is evaluating your extension before making a decision to install it. This is your chance to impress the masses of PostgreSQL developers. Don't be shy here.

Writing your extension code

Put your SQL code in the file that was provided for you in `myextension/sql/myextension.sql`. This file should contain all of the objects that make up your extension.

```
/* myextension.sql */

-- complain if script is sourced in psql, rather than via CREATE
EXTENSION
\echo Use "CREATE EXTENSION myextension" to load this file. \quit

CREATE FUNCTION feed_the_hungry() ...
```

You can provide any additional SQL files in the same directory for maintaining versions as described in the *Extension versions* section. Anything named *.sql that is located in this directory will be included in the distribution.

Creating the package

To ultimately submit our extension to the PostgreSQL Extension Network, we need to package all the files into a single zip file. Assuming we're following good practices, and we're keeping all of our source code in a handy Git repository, we can create the package through a simple `git` command. Try this one on for size:

```
git archive --format zip --prefix=myextension-0.0.1/ \
    --output ~/Desktop/myextension-0.0.1.zip master
```

This command will create a package for you that is suitable for submission to the PostgreSQL Extension Network. All we need to do now is submit it.

Submitting the package to PGXN

Now that you have a nice ZIP file in hand, you can go to the PostgreSQL Extension Network and make your accomplishment available to the community.

1.   Start by going to `http://www.pgxn.org`:

2. At the bottom of the page is a link named **Release It**. Click on the link and you will be taken to the PGXN Manager where you should log in with the username and password that you created in the first section:

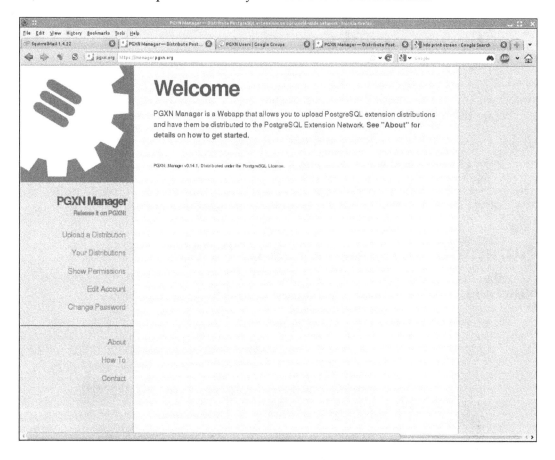

3. Click on the link **Upload a Distribution**. This will bring you to the screen where you can upload the ZIP file that you created in the *Creating the package* section:

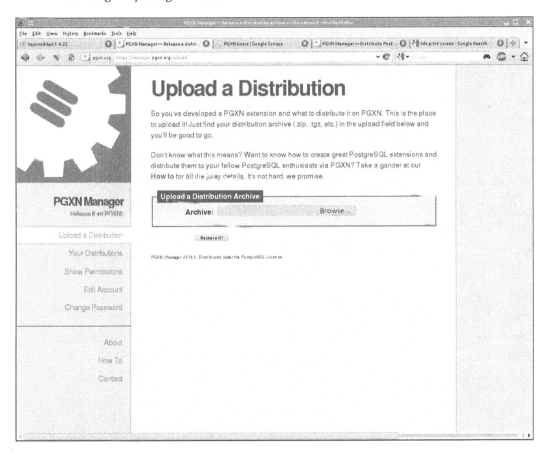

4. Browse your computer for the ZIP file and upload it to the PostgreSQL Extension Network.

That's it. Thanks again for contributing to the PostgreSQL community.

Installing an extension from PGXN

The PostgreSQL Extension Network provides a platform-independent tool to install PostgreSQL extensions. This tool is written in Python, and uses the Python installation system for distribution of itself. This is handy because the Python distribution system exists virtually on every PostgreSQL supportable platform and makes it very simple to get PostgreSQL extensions distributed to the community. The extension installer works with a single set of instructions on all targets:

```
easy_install pgxnclient
Installing pgxncli.py script to /usr/local/bin
Installing pgxn script to /usr/local/bin
Processing dependencies for pgxnclient
Finished processing dependencies for pgxnclient
```

Now you have the tools installed to manage PostgreSQL extensions provided by the PostgreSQL Extension Network.

Installing extensions is not really simple. For example, if we had a requirement to use a new `tinyint` data type, we could add it with this command:

```
pgxn install tinyint
INFO: best version: tinyint 0.1.1
INFO: saving /tmp/tmpKvr0kM/tinyint-0.1.1.zip
INFO: unpacking: /tmp/tmpKvr0kM/tinyint-0.1.1.zip
INFO: building extension
...
```

The extension is now available in the shared extensions directory on your machine. To activate it for any database, you would use the command that we started the chapter with:

```
CREATE EXTENSION tinyint;
```

You will then see the confirmation text letting you know that `tinyint` has been added:

```
CREATE EXTENSION
```

You now have the extension available for use in your local database. Enjoy!

Summary

Wow, this has been a long hard road to getting an extension configured and installed. We have used programming skills, system administrative skills, database administrative skills, and wiki editing. Along the way we saw some ruby, python, shell scripting, PL/pgSQL, and MediaWiki.

Believe it or not, this is the simplified process. Hard to imagine, eh? Well, continuous work is being done on the PostgreSQL Extension Network to further simplify this catastrophe of a development system. My thanks go out to David E. Wheeler and crew for making this new system available. As the framework now exists to help with the task, there will be dramatic improvement coming in the months and years ahead.

Now that I'm done complaining about it, this extension system is actually revolutionary. I say this because no other database platform provides any such framework at all. PostgreSQL is at the head of the pack when it comes to the ability to make changes to the basic functionality of the product. The fact that extensions can be installed and removed from the product is an indicator of how inviting PostgreSQL is to the open source community.

Extend it to do whatever you want, and they'll give you the tools to do it. This makes a PostgreSQL server the perfect framework to use for your data processing needs.

Index

Symbols

.control file
  about 218
  documentation, URL 219
#include "fmgr.h" 157
#include "postgres.h" 157
_PG_init() 187
*_to_xml function
  about 92
  variants 92

A

acquisition cost 34, 35
add_ab(PG_FUNCTION_ARGS) 157
add_func.c
  #include "fmgr.h" 157
  #include "postgres.h" 157
  about 156
  add_ab(PG_FUNCTION_ARGS) 157
  Datum 157
  PG_FUNCTION_INFO_V1(add_ab); 157
  PG_MODULE_MAGIC; 157
add_func.sql.in 160
add(int, int)
  functionality, adding 162
  multiple arguments, working with 164-170
  NULL arguments 162, 164
add_one() function 132
AFTER trigger 99, 106, 112
ALTER EXTENSION ADD command 216
ANY parameter 46
application design
  about 40
  databases, drawbacks 40

  data locality 42, 43
  encapsulation 41
arrays 69
assert
  using 150
auditing
  about 21, 22
  ways 19
audit log
  updating 109
audit trigger
  creating 102

B

backend
  synchronizing between 187
BEFORE trigger 106, 112

C

C
  additional resources 188
caching 30, 31
cancel_op() 106
cancel trigger 105
C code, writing
  guidelines 170
  memory allocation 170
C function
  add_func.c 156-158
  add_func.sql.in 160, 161
  CREATE FUNCTION add(int, int) 160
  error, reporting from 172, 173
  Makefile function 158, 159
  URL 188

INOUT parameters 78
INSTEAD OF trigger 112
integrity checks
   PL/pgSQL, using 10, 11

J

JSON
   data, returning 93-95

K

keep it simple stupid. *See* KISS
KISS 27, 28
K Nearest Neighbor. *See* KNN
KNN 30

L

licensing 36
LOG (and COMMERROR) 173
log function 143
log_min_messages 120
looping syntax
   URL 59
loops
   with counters 58, 59
Low cost of acquisition. *See* low cost of
      failure
low cost of failure 35

M

Makefile file 220
Makefile function 158-160
Master-slave replication 199
memory allocation
   about 170
   files, including 171, 172
   palloc(), using 171
   pfree(), using 171
   public symbol names 172
   structures, zero-filling 171
memset() 171
metadata
   providing, for extension 226-230
mid function 51
Multi-master replication 200

myfunc function 88
mysetfunc(); function 87
MySQL
   URL 37

N

NEW record, modifying
   trigger, timestamping 107
NOTICE 173
NULL propagation 117

O

object identifier (OID) 139
OLD, NEW variable 112
OpenFTS 216
operators
   used, for data comparisons 14
OUT parameters 78

P

package
   creating 231
   submitting, to PGXN 231-233
palloc()
   about 183
   using 171
part_func() 205
Pentaho Data Integration (kettle) 39
Pentaho Report Server 39
PERFORM command
   versus SELECT command 62
pfree()
   about 183
   using 171
pgAdmin3
   about 39, 44
   installing 122
pgFoundry
   about 188
   URL 122, 188
PG_FUNCTION_INFO_V1(add_ab); 157
PG_MODULE_MAGIC; 157
PGXN
   extension, installing from 234
   package, submitting 231-233

Thank you for buying
PostgreSQL Server Programming

About Packt Publishing

Packt, pronounced 'packed', published its first book "*Mastering phpMyAdmin for Effective MySQL Management*" in April 2004 and subsequently continued to specialize in publishing highly focused books on specific technologies and solutions.

Our books and publications share the experiences of your fellow IT professionals in adapting and customizing today's systems, applications, and frameworks. Our solution based books give you the knowledge and power to customize the software and technologies you're using to get the job done. Packt books are more specific and less general than the IT books you have seen in the past. Our unique business model allows us to bring you more focused information, giving you more of what you need to know, and less of what you don't.

Packt is a modern, yet unique publishing company, which focuses on producing quality, cutting-edge books for communities of developers, administrators, and newbies alike. For more information, please visit our website: www.packtpub.com.

About Packt Open Source

In 2010, Packt launched two new brands, Packt Open Source and Packt Enterprise, in order to continue its focus on specialization. This book is part of the Packt Open Source brand, home to books published on software built around Open Source licences, and offering information to anybody from advanced developers to budding web designers. The Open Source brand also runs Packt's Open Source Royalty Scheme, by which Packt gives a royalty to each Open Source project about whose software a book is sold.

Writing for Packt

We welcome all inquiries from people who are interested in authoring. Book proposals should be sent to author@packtpub.com. If your book idea is still at an early stage and you would like to discuss it first before writing a formal book proposal, contact us; one of our commissioning editors will get in touch with you.

We're not just looking for published authors; if you have strong technical skills but no writing experience, our experienced editors can help you develop a writing career, or simply get some additional reward for your expertise.

open source
community experience distilled

PUBLISHING

PostgreSQL 9 Admin Cookbook

ISBN: 978-1-84951-028-8   Paperback: 360 pages

Solve real-world PostgreSQL problems with over 100 simple yet incredibly effective recipes

1. Administer and maintain a healthy database

2. Monitor your database ensuring that it performs as quickly as possible

3. Tips for backup and recovery of your database

PostgreSQL 9.0 High Performance

ISBN: 978-1-84951-030-1   Paperback: 468 pages

Accelerate your PostgreSQL system and avoid the common pitfalls that can slow it down

1. Learn the right techniques to obtain optimal PostgreSQL database performance, from initial design to routine maintenance

2. Discover the techniques used to scale successful database installations

3. Avoid the common pitfalls that can slow your system down

4. Filled with advice about what you should be doing; how to build experimental databases to explore performance topics, and then move what you've learned into a production database environment

Please check **www.PacktPub.com** for information on our titles

Instant PostgreSQL Starter

ISBN: 978-1-78216-756-3   Paperback: 48 pages

Discover how to get started using PostgreSQL with minimum hassle!

1. Learn something new in an Instant! A short, fast, focused guide delivering immediate results

2. Get your database online, back it up, and make it useful as quickly as possible

3. Discover how you can utilize PostgreSQL's simple and dependable backup mechanism

Instant PostgreSQL Backup and Restore How-to

ISBN: 978-1-78216-910-9   Paperback: 54 pages

A step-by-step guide to backing up and restoring your database using safe, efficient, and proven recipes

1. Learn something new in an Instant! A short, fast, focused guide delivering immediate results

2. Back up and restore PostgreSQL databases

3. Use built-in tools to create simple backups

4. Restore the easy way with internal commands

5. Cut backup and restore time with advanced techniques

Please check **www.PacktPub.com** for information on our titles